Reserve or Renew Online

at

www.pbjclibrary.org/catalog

D1329653

P.   ,y ,stem
200 East 8th Ave.
Pine Bluff, AR 71801

DATE DUE

GAYLORD

PRINTED IN U.S.A.

In the Eye of Hurricane Andrew   *The Florida History and Culture Series*

Florida A&M University, Tallahassee
Florida Atlantic University, Boca Raton
Florida Gulf Coast University, Ft. Myers
Florida International University, Miami
Florida State University, Tallahassee
University of Central Florida, Orlando
University of Florida, Gainesville
University of North Florida, Jacksonville
University of South Florida, Tampa
University of West Florida, Pensacola

The Florida History and Culture Series
Edited by Raymond Arsenault and Gary R. Mormino

In the Eye of Hurricane Andrew

Eugene F. Provenzo, Jr., and Asterie Baker Provenzo

University Press of Florida
Gainesville · Tallahassee · Tampa · Boca Raton
Pensacola · Orlando · Miami · Jacksonville · Ft. Myers

07 06 05 04 03 02   6 5 4 3 2 1

Photo credits: All the photographs are from the National Oceanographic and
Atmospheric Administration's Historic National Weather Service Collection. They
are available online at http://www.photolib.noaa.gov/historic/nws/index.hyml.

Library of Congress Cataloging-in-Publication Data
Provenzo, Eugene F.
In the eye of Hurricane Andrew / Eugene F. Provenzo, Jr., and Asterie Baker
Provenzo.
p. cm. — (The Florida history and culture series)
Includes bibliographical references.
ISBN 0-8130-2566-4
1. Hurricane Andrew, 1992. 2. Hurricanes—Florida—Miami-Dade County.
3. Disaster relief—Florida—Miami-Dade County. 4. Hurricane protection—
Florida—Miami-Dade County. I. Provenzo, Asterie Baker. II. Title. III. Series.
HV636 1992.F676 2002
363.34'922'09759—dc21 2002016577

The University Press of Florida is the scholarly publishing agency for the State
University System of Florida, comprising Florida A&M University, Florida Atlantic
University, Florida Gulf Coast University, Florida International University, Florida
State University, University of Central Florida, University of Florida, University
of North Florida, University of South Florida, and University of West Florida.

University Press of Florida
15 Northwest 15th Street
Gainesville, FL 32611–2079
http://www.upf.com

For Gene's colleagues at the University of Miami,
and their families, who lost their homes and yet had
the courage to rebuild their lives and go on with their work:

Scott Baldwin
Jack Croghan
Charles Hanneman
Charles Mangrum
Shawn Post
Marilyn de Narvaez
Paul Dee
Joseph Signorile

Contents

Foreword

In the Eye of Hurricane Andrew is the twenty-second volume in a series devoted to the study of Florida history and culture. During the past half century, the burgeoning population and increasing national and international visibility of Florida have sparked a great deal of popular interest in the state's past, present, and future. As the favorite destination of countless tourists and as the new home for millions of retirees and other migrants, modern Florida has become a demographic, political, and cultural bellwether. Unfortunately, the quantity and quality of the literature on Florida's distinctive heritage and character have not kept pace with the Sunshine State's enhanced status. In an effort to remedy this situation—to provide an accessible and attractive format for the publication of Florida-related books—the University Press of Florida has established the Florida History and Culture Series.

As coeditors of the series, we are committed to the creation of an eclectic but carefully crafted set of books that will provide the field of Florida studies with a new focus and that will encourage Florida researchers and writers to consider the broader implications and context of their work. The series will continue to include standard academic monographs, works of synthesis, memoirs, and anthologies. And while the series will feature books of historical interest, we encourage the submission of manuscripts on Florida's environment, politics, literature, and popular and material culture for inclusion in the series. We want each book to retain a distinct personality and voice, but at the same time we hope to foster a sense of community and collaboration among Florida scholars.

With *In the Eye of Hurricane Andrew,* Eugene F. Provenzo, Jr., and Asterie Baker Provenzo retell an extraordinary chapter in the history of modern Florida. More than a book about a hurricane, *In the Eye of Hurricane Andrew* weaves together the myriad themes that unite and divide Floridians: the role of the mass media, natural disasters, human foibles, local and national politics, and the fragile yet remarkably resilient and enchanting South Florida environment. The book is both intensely personal (the authors teach and live in South Florida) and highly professional (the authors and a team of student researchers interviewed nearly a hundred individuals about the trauma of August 1992 and help place the event in perspective).

The history of Florida is littered (literally and figuratively) with the consequences of hurricanes. Tons of Aztec gold, Inca silver, and skeletons lie on the bottom of the Florida Straits. Scholars have come to recognize how important natural disasters can be and how such events bear the handprints of humans. Hurricanes have served as seminal events in Florida history. The hurricane of 1926 pricked the deflating South Florida land boom. In 1928 a vicious hurricane killed several thousand residents who died as the result of a tidal wave sweeping across Lake Okeechobee, the worst human calamity in modern Florida history.

Hurricane Andrew was, quite simply and astonishingly, the most costly natural catastrophe in American history. The events of August 24, 1992, fill a doomsday book of grim statistics: 1.4 million families left without electricity; more than 100,000 private homes damaged or destroyed; 250,000 Floridians left homeless; and a price tag tabulated at between $20 and $30 billion.

If the financial and physical costs were staggering, so was the toll on Floridians' psyches. The Provenzos deftly weave memoirs and recorded experiences with text to provide a riveting study. *In the Eye of Hurricane Andrew* portrays South Floridians at their worst (price gougers, "roofers from hell," and feckless politicians) but also introduces a cast of unlikely heroes (meteorologists, Jehovah's Witnesses, and Boy Scouts). Readers will draw their own conclusions as to the lessons of Andrew, but this is a book every Floridian should read.

Raymond Arsenault and Gary R. Mormino
Series Editors

Preface

The sky was a murky, heavy gray, and it rained softly most of the weekend of August 15, 1992. Even the locals found the weather unusual for August in Washington, D.C. As visitors from Miami, we found it chilly enough to wear raincoats. We were in the capital to work on a project at the National Museum of American Art. On Monday, August 17, we began working with curators and staff from the Office of Publications at the museum. That was the day Andrew formed as a tropical storm. After two long days of work, on Wednesday morning, August 19, a few hours before our flight back to Miami, we were standing around discussing when we could get a revision of the manuscript we were working on back to the publication staff. They wanted it by the following Monday. "No problem," Asterie said, "unless Andrew becomes a hurricane." "What do you mean?" they asked. "There's a tropical storm out there," she replied. "It's called Andrew."

When Hurricane Andrew struck our neighborhood in Miami, winds were recorded at the National Hurricane Center, about a mile from our

Long lines waiting for ice after Hurricane Andrew. (Image ID: wea00559)

home, at 164 miles per hour, and then the wind gauge broke. Living through the storm was the most frightening and exhausting thing either of us has ever experienced.

Gene began informally interviewing people almost immediately after the storm. For him, it was a way of coping, of trying to understand the enormity of what had happened. He also realized that it was an extraordinary opportunity—a time to witness history. All too often, amid the struggle and crisis of a major event or disaster, no one is there to note what is taking place, to create a record of what happened. To reach beyond the newspaper accounts and "eyewitness" news reports of local and national television seemed imperative.

The project was continued as a collaborative effort with graduate students and undergraduate honors students at the University of Miami during the 1992–93 school year. Nearly everyone who conducted interviews had lived through the immediate terror of the storm. The lives of many of the students were dramatically changed forever by Andrew. This project seemed to be a way of coping for them, too. The interviews are a testament to their determination to keep up with their schoolwork and to their desire to contribute to the rebuilding effort of the community. Interviewees were selected, to some degree, from the friends and acquaintances of the students. As a result, interviewees were often, although by no means primarily, from the southern part of Miami-Dade County, where most of the students lived, or were associated with the University of Miami. Of the ninety-two interviewees, fifteen were students, staff, or faculty at the university. Some of these, however, were interviewed for their research expertise (such as Harold Wanless, associate professor of geology), not because of their association with the university.

This book is not intended to be a definitive history of Hurricane Andrew. It is a book about a selected group of South Floridians, about survivors and rescuers and heroes and villains. It is a record of the experiences of some of the people who were caught up in the abnormal conditions created by what many believe was the worst natural disaster in the history of the United States.

In addition to the interview sources, we have drawn on newspaper accounts and related reports. These works, in particular the articles describing the storm and its aftermath in the *Miami Herald,* provided an invaluable resource to put the interviews in context. As an appendix, we have included an expanded version of the comprehensive bibliography of Hurricane Andrew created by our former colleague William E. Brown, Jr., who was head of the Archives and Special Collections Department, Otto G. Richter Library, at the University of Miami. *In the Eye of Hurricane Andrew* originally appeared in the *Bulletin of Bibliography* to mark the fifth anniversary of the storm. It has since been updated and now includes more than three hundred books, pamphlets, and conference proceedings; local, state and federal government reports; maps, video recordings, dissertations, and even novels. We thank the *Bulletin of Bibliography* (vol. 55, no. 1, pp. 25–33) for permission to reprint Brown's work.

This book is a unique collaboration between the two authors and the students who collected the oral history interviews. We want especially to thank the students for their enthusiasm and for their excellent work in collecting most of the interviews. Transcripts and tapes of all the interviews collected are permanently preserved and available for use in the Archives and Special Collections Department, Otto G. Richter Library, University of Miami, Coral Gables, Florida. Finally, we owe a special thanks to all of the people who were willing to talk with the students and us. It is, after all, their story.

Asterie and Eugene Provenzo

HURRICANE ANDREW
AUG 23, 1992
155 MPH   922 MB

"It's Going to Be Very, Very Bad"

1

Hurricane Andrew struck South Florida early on Monday morning, August 24, 1992. Immediately following the storm, 1.4 million families were left without electricity. More than 107,800 private homes were damaged or destroyed; 49,000 of those were left uninhabitable. More than 1,600 public housing units were also damaged or destroyed.[1] As a result, more than 250,000 people were left homeless. Damages were estimated at between $20 and $30 billion dollars. From a financial point of view, Hurricane Andrew was the most costly natural disaster in modern American

Visible satellite image of Hurricane Andrew during its period of maximum intensity over the Bahamas, August 23, 1992. (Image ID: wea00520)

history. From a psychological and social point of view, the storm was similarly unprecedented.

Historically, Florida has suffered the impact of hurricanes more than any other part of the country. Of the 151 major hurricanes to have struck the United States between 1900 and 1989, 54 hit Florida; Texas and Louisiana were second and third with 36 and 24 storms respectively. Four of the five most powerful storms of the century—including Hurricane Andrew—hit somewhere along the Florida coast.[2]

Andrew was a category 4 hurricane. The only storm to hit Florida with stronger winds was the category 5 hurricane that struck Monroe County and the Florida Keys in 1935.[3] The 1935 storm, although responsible for the deaths of four hundred people, affected fewer individuals because it struck a relatively unpopulated area. No storm of the size and magnitude of Hurricane Andrew had ever directly hit a major urban area like Dade County.

According to Bob Sheets, then the director of the National Hurricane Center, Hurricane Andrew was the third-strongest storm on record: "It's by far the most devastating of any hurricane that I've looked at. I've looked at them all since 1965. Even Camille. Camille was stronger. Camille had the same kind of devastation, but much more concentrated than what we have here. We're essentially talking about three hundred square miles of devastation for an area fifteen miles inland. The only reason it stopped fifteen miles inland is because that's where the property stopped. That's where people stopped."[4] In fact, the storm continued across the state to the west coast of Florida, leaving a wide trail of devastation and destruction through the Everglades. Hitting the state's east coast as a category 4 storm, Hurricane Andrew entered the Gulf of Mexico as a category 3 hurricane—and began to gain strength again over open water.

Until Andrew, the worst storm to hit Dade County was the category 4 hurricane that struck Miami Beach and Miami on September 18, 1926. Although both Andrew and the 1926 storm were category 4 hurricanes, the 1926 hurricane was very different from Andrew, cutting a path of destruction sixty miles wide from Moore Haven on Lake Okeechobee south to Homestead. While the hurricane in 1926 was "huge, slow and sloppy," Andrew has been described as being "like a killer pit bull—small, strong, quick and incredibly mean."[5]

Hurricane Andrew's eye measured between eight and ten miles across. Maximum winds recorded for the storm were 169 miles per hour. Sustained winds, which over water were 150 miles per hour, were reduced to 140 miles per hour when they struck land. The maximum storm surge recorded for the storm was 16.9 feet.[6] Whirlwinds or vortices in the wall of the hurricane's eye may have created winds as high as 200 miles per hour.[7]

A few facts and comparisons may help to put the storm in perspective. The number of people left homeless by Andrew was greater than the population of St. Petersburg, Florida, and approximately the size of the population of Las Vegas, Nevada. The amount of garbage generated by the storm in a single night was equal to the normal projected landfill for Dade County for the next thirty years.[8]

Before the Storm

Hurricane Andrew began as a lazy tropical depression located to the southeast of Florida. It didn't gain much attention until Saturday morning, August 21, 1992. At that time, the storm was eight hundred miles east of Miami with winds of about seventy-five miles per hour. As Saturday progressed, South Floridians became more and more aware of the possibility of a major hurricane hitting their communities.

Although Florida has been struck by more hurricanes than any other region of the continental United States, most people living in South Florida in 1992 had never experienced a hurricane. The last major hurricane to hit the area was Donna in 1964.

To many people, the very idea of a hurricane was not only totally new but also a little unreal. Vida Pernick, a realtor living in Coral Gables, for example, recalled how the Saturday before the storm was a beautiful day: "The skies were blue, not a sign of rain. I remember sitting around the pool and saying to myself that it was almost impossible to think that a hurricane is coming straight at us on such a beautiful day." Pernick, however, like many others in the community, began to make preparations for the storm. On Saturday, she took outdoor furniture into her house and removed anything she "thought might fly," as the storm headed straight for the coast.[9]

She was not the only person who felt that the threat of the storm was somehow unreal. Alexis Martinez, a student at Barry University and a part-time clerk at United Parcel Service, recalled that on Saturday he went out on a friend's boat: "We spent the whole day out on [the] sea. The sea was beautiful. It was calm; the sun was shining; [it was] very hot. There was really no indication that we were threatened by a hurricane approaching South Florida."[10]

Many people went on with their regular routines throughout the day, becoming concerned about the storm only as they saw friends and neighbors taking emergency precautions and stocking up on hurricane supplies. Alicia Jeffers, a hospital administrator living in the southern part of the county, for example, recalled that she did not take the storm too seriously: "I didn't realize that it was a serious thing. . . . I happened to have gone shopping that Saturday. It was a regular routine, grocery shopping, and I saw people getting bottles of water. In fact, the water shelf was empty. . . . I realized people were starting to get a little antsy about it, kind of saying, 'Well, maybe . . .' So, I did the same thing, I said, 'Maybe I should get this, maybe I should get that,' and I started to prepare."[11]

James White, a psychologist at the Family and Adolescent Development Center, first heard about the possibility of a storm while visiting his mother in Pennsylvania. Rushing back to Florida on Saturday afternoon, he immediately took a limousine to his apartment on Miami Beach. "As soon as I dropped my luggage in my living room, I heard a knock on my door and it was [the] maintenance service and there were about five people . . . and they came in and started boarding up; . . . they took all the furniture off the balcony and put it in the living room and they put tape on the windows and so forth."[12]

Some people could not get off work on Saturday to buy hurricane supplies. By Saturday evening, lines were beginning to form throughout the county outside supermarkets such as Publix and Winn Dixie. Many found the lines so long, and the people so rude, that they gave up and went home empty-handed. James Mooney, executive director of Metro Dade's Department of Youth and Family Development, who had just returned from a trip to Tampa on Saturday, recalled: "When I got back, my wife and I were going to dinner and she said, 'There's a storm out there.' I hadn't listened to the radio and I didn't believe it and then . . . the waiter talked about the storm, the pending storm, the storm warning . . . and then, we stopped at Publix to pick up some supplies and it looked like the storm had hit Publix! So that's when I realized that it was a very strong possibility it was going to hit."[13]

Eve McNanamy, a clinical psychologist, says she realized on Saturday that the storm would probably hit Miami and began to make the necessary preparations. "I found someone who was willing to put up my steel storm shutters. We hurriedly went to the grocery store and purchased as many batteries and as much canned food and other things that we could possibly find, although there were so many people at the supermarket that it was difficult to find many of the items, and then we put gasoline in the car, came home, and began to hope for the best."[14]

By Saturday evening, more people began tuning in their television sets, wondering whether or not this was really going to be "the big one" that had been predicted for years. Alicia Jeffers became convinced late Saturday evening that the hurricane might actually hit: "Around midnight is when I really took it serious, because Bryan Norcross on Channel 4 showed pictures and it seemed to be on a very steady course. At that point, my husband was asleep, so was my daughter. . . . I awakened my husband and I told him, 'I'm going to get gas, just in case this thing does hit. You know, we're in the evacuation zone.'"[15]

For many people involved with emergency support services, Saturday was a day of careful planning and preparation. Lawrence Moose, who worked at the Greater Miami Chapter of the American Red Cross, had planned to go to the beach with his sister, who was visiting from out of town. Instead, he found himself trying to get his apartment secure and bringing in supplies for his sister in case she was unable to leave town before the storm. At 5:00 P.M. on Saturday he reported to the local Red Cross chapter offices, where he and his co-workers began making preparations "for shipments of goods to shelters; . . . there were still decisions being made about which shelters should be opened. We still weren't sure if the hurricane was coming. The shelters are divided up into different levels, and we weren't sure which ones were going to be activated because we weren't sure which areas were going to be targeted. So we were on the phone with Emergency Management, who makes that call about which areas get evacuated." Moose and his co-workers at the Red Cross continued making preparations into the early hours on Sunday. "We were also on the phone with our primary vendors to supply shelters with food and water and milk and stuff like that; . . . the reason I say it's kind of a blur is from six o'clock till about two in the morning we were making vendor contacts and getting updates on the latest information from the weather folks, from Emergency Management, about which shelters they thought were going to be opened."[16]

Florence T. Goldstein was a shelter volunteer. She was planning to go to her son's house in Davie (about 20 miles north in Broward County) when the Red Cross called her and asked her go to North Miami Beach Senior High school, which was one of the shelters. Her job was to sign people in as they came into the shelter. "I stayed three days and three nights. We had quite a crowd."[17] Not expecting the storm to be as bad as it was, she took only her pocketbook with her, no change of clothing.

At the University of Miami, long-standing emergency procedures were set in motion for boarding up windows and taking care of people who might be stranded on the campus. Despite careful pre-planning, Edward T. Foote II, the university's president, found himself asking questions such as: "Do we have enough water? Do we have enough food?" As the likelihood of the hurricane hitting Coral Gables became a greater and greater possibility, Foote explained that he "was as comfortable as I could be under the circumstances. But that wasn't all that comfortable because, as the hours wore on, it was clear that this was a very, very serious storm, and you can never know how closely the preparations will match the facts, and it was the facts that we didn't know."[18]

As Hurricane Andrew came closer and closer to South Florida, waiting to see if the storm would actually hit was probably hardest for South Floridians who had to be in another part of the country while their friends and loved ones prepared for the storm back home. Irene Baljet, an American Airlines flight attendant, had to work the weekend of the storm. "I was in Allentown, Pennsylvania, and I watched the weather channel and by that time Saturday night, already it was very obvious that this was going to be a very bad, very big hurricane—very bad for the area. . . . The company did not want any airplanes at the Miami airport because of the impending [storm], so they canceled the Atlanta-Miami [run]." Baljet and many others like her had no way of getting back to Miami to help their families and friends: "My husband and my daughter . . . were able to prepare the house, the yard. I have a million plants in my yard, so my daughter worked very hard to secure them and put them in a safe place, but the captain and a couple of other flight attendants were single people and they had no one to tie down their houses. So there was a great deal of anxiety among the crew."[19]

By Sunday morning, television and radio stations warned that final preparations had to be made by nightfall. Early Sunday morning was too late for some people, who went to Home Depot and were not even allowed in the parking lot because the store was already out of plywood. All day Sunday, people throughout South Florida battened down their houses and made runs for whatever supplies they could find in the local supermarkets and stores. By the afternoon, most grocery stores, hardware stores, and lumberyards were empty of any useful items. When they could not obtain the necessary supplies, people started making do by clearing rooms that had unshielded windows and moving furniture and electrical appliances off the floor in case of flooding.

Margaret Sowell, a registered nurse who worked at Deering Hospital in South Dade, recalled how she and her family got ready for the storm on Sunday. They secured all the windows in her house, cleaned the bathtub and filled it with water, and got everything out of the way that "might fly around."[20]

At the northern end of town, Ronald V. Ponton, a Jehovah's Witness minister, tried to help older friends and neighbors who needed assistance. "We made some calls concerning some older friends, but they were being taken care of by some other friends. But here in the neighborhood on either side of us were families with no husbands or father, so we were able to help both sides of our neighbors in getting their awnings down, getting everything secure and getting them all prepared so that they could weather the storm also."[21]

Soloman Graham, the supervisor of the physical plant for Campus Sports and Recreation at the University of Miami and a longtime resident of South Miami, said that he tied down lights in his backyard "and put the shutters down on the house; . . . I'm not into that taping the windows, so with the shutters down you wouldn't need the windows taped. There are a couple of windows that don't have shutters, but they're on the west side of the house. So, even with the windows being taped, I think a couple of those got crashed—not the windows on the house, but on the car shed. And most of the junk I have in the backyard, like barrels, and wheelbarrows, and drums, I put all those under the shed."[22]

Paul Shaffer, a Foreign Service officer who lived south of Soloman Graham, was convinced that the storm would hit the area once it had crossed over the Bahamas. When he got up on Sunday, his thought was:

> "We are in trouble." I think that when it crossed the Bahamas it was clocked at 120 miles per hour, and judging from my old Mexican science attaché days, I figured we were in for a lot of trouble. So the first thing I did was go out and try to find plywood, which was a disaster. We finally located some that was not as thick or as strong as I had wanted. . . . I ended up nailing those with uncut nails, from a neighbor. . . . There were no nails to be found. So we ended up doing the north and east ends of the house—it's all we had wood for— because I knew it would be coming from the east and from the north. . . . We closed all the windows. We locked all the windows. We put the curtains across the windows. We flattened down the shades. We took everything off the walls. I was afraid that if the wind did come in, it was going to blow everything off the walls. So we very carefully took all these things down and tucked them away inside dresser drawers, inside closets, inside cedar chests, inside anything, anything that we could fit. We took everything off countertops, off tabletops. Anything that was light, we took off the floor. We took all the pool things inside the garage or inside the house. We moved furniture around towards the wall so that it wouldn't blow away.[23]

Shaffer's attempt to batten down his house was typical of many people's throughout the county. Rodester Brandon, the bandleader at Homestead Senior High School, recalled that on Sunday he bought plywood and started boarding up his house.

> I . . . came home and drilled holes in the wall and put anchors in the building and bolted the plywood to the window; . . . each window took

about an hour to do. . . . That whole Sunday was, like, a lot of hard work. Finally, about 4:00 P.M., I just stopped, stopped trying to prepare, and I said, "Well, you know, if this thing is coming this way and it is going to be that bad, just let it go. . . ." My neighbor down the street, who works at Miami Dade, . . . is an oceanographer. I went down to talk to him and I said, "What do you think about this hurricane coming around?" And he said, "Listen, if this thing becomes a category 4 hurricane" (which it did by about 3 P.M.), "then I am not going to stay."

And then, right down the street from me also . . . is a guy by the name of Bass who works for the hurricane service. He flies right into the center of the eye, and he says, "No way, don't stay, leave!" At that time, I said that I'm out of here!

So I was going to go out to my mother's house. Around 6 P.M. or so we got there, and she had her shutters on her windows and everything, so we said okay, we are going to stay here in her house. I looked at the television, and they said that it was 140–mile-an-hour winds and [that] by the time it got over the Gulf Stream, it was going to be 160 miles an hour. And I said no way! . . . I said this is no place to be. . . . I kind of related it to the fact that, you know, the way I would drive my car. I won't go 80 miles an hour in my car. . . . The hurricane was twice as fast. . . . So at about 8:30 P.M. we decided to get into the car and go to Lakeland [over 200 miles north in central Florida].[24]

At the Key Biscayne Marina, Mike Puller, a charter fisherman, described how he "spent the day before the storm just doubling up all the lines and leaving enough line for the surge to make sure the boats couldn't hit anything."[25]

According to Mike Brescher, a dockmaster at the Crandon Park Marina on Key Biscayne, a great deal of confusion developed as people tried to take their boats out of the bay and up the Miami River where they would be safer. Bridges across the river were not supposed to be locked down until the wind speed hit thirty-five miles per hour. Sunday proved to be a beautiful day—yet people trying to take their boats upriver were sent back. According to Brescher: "The bridges just locked down. They weren't allowed to go through. And everybody who tried to get up the river got sent back.

They had reserved spaces but couldn't get through, so they had to come back. So we did the best we could. They anchored them in the Marine Stadium. Meanwhile these people had sent people up the roads to meet them up there to drive them back. There was so much confusion." Brescher said the rumor around the docks was that the shipping interests on the river saw to it that the bridges were locked down early so that smaller boats could not come up river. "We found out that there was a lot of pressure coming from shipping, that basically they didn't want to worry about all of the small boats . . . on the Miami River blocking the river. Because if they sunk in the river, they couldn't get the shipping in and out. Meanwhile they were shipping stuff within the next two days."[26]

Among the most difficult places to prepare for the storm were tourist attractions such as the Miami Seaquarium, Parrot Jungle, and Metrozoo. Damien Kong, who worked with his wife at Metrozoo, stayed with his children and prepared his home for the storm while his wife, the lead bird keeper at the zoo, secured the animals in her care. According to Kong, the zookeepers at Metrozoo "tried to prepare as much as they could. They secured all the animals that they thought could get blown away. They put all the animals in their night houses, in the back areas. . . . A lot of people said, "Well, why didn't you put up all the birds in the aviary?" Well, we don't have cages for three hundred birds. That's just not a physical possibility. There's also 1.7 acres, so you can't just go out and catch all those birds."[27]

Evacuation Plans and Decisions to Leave

In flood zones, which included most of the areas along the coast, people prepared their homes as best they could and began to evacuate to shelters or stay with friends who were in safer areas. Paul Dee, then general counsel at the University of Miami, took his invalid mother-in-law to Baptist Hospital. His wife remained with her mother, while he and his son stayed in a motel several miles west of their Old Cutler house. Dee's precautions probably saved him and his family.

Paul Shaffer and his wife also decided that staying in their house, which was in an evacuation zone, would be foolish. They chose to leave Dade County and go to stay with relatives in Clearwater, on the west coast of Central Florida:

Laurie and I have done a lot of things, dangerous things, in our life together. Now we have three kids, and we decided it was okay to do dangerous things in our life, by ourselves, but not with the kids. And since my brother lives in Clearwater, we decided, well, we'll go up there and spend the night and then come back the next day, after the storm has just dumped a bunch of water and then gone. We weren't thinking in terms of destroyed homes.

We were hearing horror stories on Sunday about how clogged certain highways were, and certain exit ways were. People were saying, "Don't get out on the road because you'll join all these people." I watched the news, Bryan Norcross, and it looked like it was going to hit straight on the house. I decided it was worth the risk, jumping in the car and going across as fast as possible, and getting out of here. I figured with about twelve hours to spare, we could probably get out. We packed—actually, I should say Laurie packed—the car with food and extra clothes, and our important papers.[28]

Alicia Jeffers was also one of the thousands who decided to evacuate their homes and drive due north to get out of the path of Hurricane Andrew. Together with her husband and daughter she headed up to the central part of the state. "The drive up was incredible. Our biggest fear, or my fear, was to get stuck with all the people [on the turnpike]. They had evacuated Fort Lauderdale as well, half a million people, plus those of us in South Dade on the east side. So my fear was getting stuck on the highway and the storm hitting in Fort Lauderdale and we couldn't go back or forward. That was my big fear. But that didn't happen. They turned the turnpike into all north lanes by noon. We left at 10 A.M."[29] All of the major arteries leading north from Miami were jammed for 120 miles. Jeffers and her husband, Lennox, finally arrived in Kissimmee at 9:00 P.M. on Sunday night—the drive, which normally takes three hours, had taken eleven.

As early as Sunday morning, county officials had pleaded for all available medical personnel to volunteer their services at the local evacuation centers. All women in their final term of pregnancy were requested to go to Jackson Memorial Hospital, where a special medical support team had been assembled. By 10:00 P.M. Sunday evening, the halls of Jackson Memorial Hospital were lined with pregnant women. Most of them were without their families and had no idea how long they would be at the hospital.

Evacuation posed a serious problem for many hospitals and prison facilities. John Cleveland, the medical director of the Memorial Hospital satellite programs, found himself having to move entire facilities to more secure areas. At the Perdue Medical Center on Old Cutler Road in the southern part of the county, Cleveland supervised the transfer of 160 patients to the Human Resources Health Center on Northwest Twenty-second Avenue. The evacuation began on Sunday morning and continued until about four o'clock in the afternoon. Buses were used for transport, as well as vans equipped to carry people in wheelchairs. The most seriously ill were transported by ambulance.

The clinic at the county jail, which was under Cleveland's supervision, was shut and the jail itself locked down. Nobody came in and nobody went out. The Liberty City Clinic with which Cleveland was also affiliated simply closed, and it did not reopen until the Thursday after the storm.

At the Human Resources Health Center, Cleveland had to deal with about 320 people, including those who were brought from another facility in Cutler Ridge in the southern part of the county and those who were already residents at the facility. Space was at a premium: "We had people in the hallways, we had people in a wing that had not been used yet that had recently been built, and we had people in the dining room."[30]

For many parents with disabled children, preparations for the hurricane were particularly trying. Pat Warren's adult son Andy had muscular dystrophy and was dependent on a ventilator. Once she realized that the storm was likely to hit, she and her husband "started thinking of how we were going to get power. We charged the batteries; . . . we don't have a generator. We had enough power to last for two days, possibly three. We decided we were going to stay here [home] and stick it out." As it became clear that the storm was going to be worse than expected, Warren and her husband decided to get Andy to a local hospital: "At 10:00 A.M. on Sunday, I took him in—he and his nurse [Andy has around-the-clock nursing care] and myself. We went to Baptist [Hospital] and, of course, at Baptist they wanted to put him in the Intensive Care Unit because he is on a ventilator, and then hook him up to monitors. All that is ridiculous because he is stable and doesn't need all that. So anyway, we decided to take him to the shelter in the rehab center at Baptist. . . . They were very nice there. They gave him food and anything he wanted. So they gave us a bed and [electric] power."[31]

At 8:00 P.M. Sunday, the National Hurricane Center announced that Hurricane Andrew was 185 miles east of Miami. Kate Hale, Dade County emergency director, was telling everyone to have enough supplies to be able to operate for one week on their own. More than 180,000 people were evacuated to emergency shelters, away from low flood zones. Most of these shelters were public schools. Bus service stopped at 10:00 P.M. By 10:30 P.M., police were telling everyone to get off the streets. At almost the last possible moment, Emergency Management officials realized that a large number of homeless people living in cardboard shelters underneath a downtown freeway had not been evacuated. At 11:59 P.M. four buses were sent out to take them to local shelters.

Expectations

Almost no one in the community anticipated how severe the storm would be. Martin J. Carney, director of Financial Assistance Services at the University of Miami, explained: "I don't think anyone expected the damage to the extent that we received, due to the fact that so many people are transplanted from other locations throughout the country and hadn't experienced a hurricane. And certainly nothing as devastating as Andrew. Nobody had any idea of the ramifications, so I don't think that we were as well prepared as we should have been. Of course, I don't think we could have been, not having been through it once."[32] Previous hurricane threats had failed to materialize. In 1979, for example, Hurricane David seemed to be on a direct collision course with Miami and then veered off at the last moment. As mentioned earlier, the last major hurricane to hit the South Florida area was Donna in 1964. Eve A. Koenig, an art teacher at Palmer-Trinity School who was left homeless by Andrew, thought that "the storm would be something like the previous experiences we have had with hurricane warnings where we only had a lot of rain and wind, but nothing that really caused any destruction to the homes. We absolutely did not expect the damage that we did receive from the hurricane. It was a total shock. And I would never again stay in the area, because our area was told to evacuate but I guess we just didn't realize the intensity of the storm and the resulting damage. We had no idea."[33]

Heavy winds and rain were reported from Fort Lauderdale, north of Miami, down to southern Dade County by 11:00 P.M. Television reporters described the storm as "beginning to rock-and-roll." The National Hurricane Center warned that the thrust of the hurricane would be felt for the next twelve to sixteen hours. Bryan Norcross, a meteorologist at Channel 4, WTVJ, who had taken over the lead position on the newscast, warned South Floridians: "Absolutely, there is no doubt about it, it is going to happen tonight."

Elizabeth Garcia Granados, an instructor at Miami-Dade Community College and a longtime resident of Florida, recalls questioning the predictions of the weather people. "I grew up in Florida and just assumed that they were exaggerating and that it was not going to be as serious as it turned out to be. I had no idea."[34] Howard Camner, a poet and writer, was one of the many people in Dade County who "didn't realize what kind of monster it was going to be."[35]

Besides misjudging the severity of the storm itself, most people in the community had little sense of how long they might be cut off from services such as electricity, or how much difficulty they might have obtaining groceries or other necessary items. Richard Anderson, a pest control specialist living in the Howard Drive area (Southwest 136th Street), explained that while he and his family had prepared their house for the storm, "what we did not prepare for was the time frame to be without power—so there was not enough food and water on hand. So that is something we sort of fell behind on—whether we got lazy or just didn't think it was going to hit, or be as bad as it was. It taught us a good lesson."[36]

By midnight Sunday the winds had increased to more than one hundred miles per hour. Brilliant bursts of blue-green lightning forked across the sky. What had happened to the traditional hurricane parties with beer and junk food? Perhaps too many people had heard Bryan Norcross warn, "Friends, it is going to happen now for Dade County; . . . it's going to be very, very bad."

August 24, 1992

2

By 2:00 A.M. Monday, August 24, 1992, trees had begun to topple, block-ing roads throughout the county. In our neighborhood in Coral Gables, a few blocks from the University of Miami campus, the power went out at 3:22 A.M. All over the county, lights, air-conditioners, and televisions shut off. Hurricane Andrew was about forty miles east of Miami, with winds of 140 miles per hour. Bryan Norcross, now broadcasting via radio, advised everyone to hunker down and stay put: "There is no safe place in South Florida tonight. These winds exceed the building codes."[1]

Infrared satellite image showing Hurricane Andrew as it crosses the Florida coast and makes land-fall, August 24, 1992, at Dade County, Florida. (Image ID: wea00521)

The eyewall of the storm entered Biscayne Bay at 4:28 A.M. At that time, all police and fire personnel were ordered off the streets. A short time later, at the National Hurricane Center in Coral Gables, the storm blew the Center's radar system ball off the roof. At 5:20 A.M. the wind gauge at the Hurricane Center recorded winds of 164 miles per hour—then it broke.[2]

Andrew Feldman, an employee at the Miami Seaquarium, expressed the feelings of thousands of South Floridians when he described Hurricane Andrew as the most frightening experience of his life.[3] The storm was a terrifying experience, not just for those whose homes were being destroyed around them, but also for those who weathered the storm relatively unharmed—not knowing what destruction they would find outside, not knowing how much worse it was going to get. Lisa Jacobson, an employee at Liberty Mutual Insurance Company, for example, came through the storm with no injuries and relatively little damage to her house. Despite this, she described herself as being very scared and said she prayed throughout the entire storm.[4]

Weathering Andrew

For Sergeant Michael Laughlin, a seventeen-year veteran of the Metro Dade police force, whose house on Southwest 158th Street was in the central area of the storm, experiencing Hurricane Andrew was more physically frightening than for many people:

> During the hurricane we woke up to the sound of aluminum banging. I figured my screened-in patio was being blown away. We walked outside and it was all right. When we went inside the living room, we saw that my neighbor was trying to hold the door shut. It was double doors, and I went to help him out. I have no idea how long a length of time we stayed there trying to hold those doors closed. Finally, we gave up and evacuated to the garage. We stayed in there for a while. When I first walked in, the access way to the crawl space was flapping with the wind. After being in there for a while I noticed that the ceiling of the garage right over the garage door was trying to lift off. I was afraid the garage was going to blow away with the roof. Then a

little while later I looked up through that crawl space, and I could see the lightning through there. And the only way that I could see lightning was if, in fact, I had lost part of my roof. And that was my first true moment of—I'm not going to say panic—but . . . intense fear that [it] was worse, and going to get a lot worse, than I had anticipated.[5]

Eve Koenig described an almost identical experience: "We realized that most of the windows in the house must have broken and the water was about six inches [deep], and I thought we might possibly drown in it because it kept rising up. When the storm started to diminish, my husband would go out of the bathroom to check on what was going on. Then I would hear loud crashes and I would call him and he wouldn't answer, so I would assume something had fallen on him. Then I actually went out, walking through the water to find him. You could see flashes of lightning out through the broken doors, but it was so frightening, I would not stay out there very long."[6]

Grace Laskis, a Head Start disabilities coordinator, described how she and her children were weathering the storm in an upstairs hallway of their house when suddenly the sliding glass doors on the first floor blew out:

I went downstairs and listened to the wind howling on the glass sliding doors . . . then they went. So my son and I went for the bookcases and started removing the books so we could push the cases against the broken glass doors. The funny thing was that one of the cases had my brand-new encyclopedia . . . and I kept yelling, "No, no!" My son turned to me and said, "Mom, they got to go!" We pushed the cases against the doors as the other glass doors went and the windows started to break. . . .

Suddenly, it was hopeless . . . the wind was inside the house, everything was swirling, it was unbelievable; . . . we went upstairs and the walls were shaking unbelievably, all the windows and skylights blew out, the walls and the second floor began to lift like it was paper. I said we had to get out of here . . . then we heard the train sound . . . like an actual train barreling down on the house. . . . I said, we have to go back downstairs.

Everyone was frantic. I took each of my children piggyback, covered them with a blanket, downstairs. My daughter was frantic for her cats, but they ran away. We grabbed the dog and all went into the half bathroom downstairs; . . . imagine it, two adults, three teenagers and another child and the dog in this 2 x 2 half bath. . . . We pushed blankets under the door, but we had to keep pulling it out to get some fresh air. . . . We heard things flying around outside the door. Bombs going off, it seemed . . . windows were exploding. . . . The girls were nervous and they got so sick, vomiting, everything . . . everyone on top of each other.

Finally, for Grace and her family, "things began to quiet down . . . the wind died down and it was raining."[7]

Karen Baldwin, an elementary school teacher living in the area just north of the eye of the hurricane, described how, at the height of the storm, she and her husband and teenage son barricaded themselves in a closet in a protected bedroom:

The wind was so loud that you could not talk or hear without shouting. . . . The noise level got to be eerie. To me, it was absolutely the most horrible noise that you could imagine. Everybody says it sounds like a freight train. It was much worse than a freight train, between the howling and the whistling of the wind. It was an incredible, indescribable noise. . . .

I grabbed Doug's [her son] Walkman, put the headphones on, and turned the volume up full blast, which in effect did drown out a good portion of the noise. It didn't drown it all out, but it made it that much more bearable because I was listening to a very calm voice on the radio talking people through the storm—the voice of Bryan Norcross.[8]

Madeline Martinez, from Kendall, was one of the people who called Norcross at the station. When asked what her situation was, Madeline replied: "Okay. We have a, a window broken in one of the rooms and the door's closed and they're trying to hold it back because it looks like it's going to cave in."[9]

Norcross told her: "All right, that's what you need to do . . . need to stay in that enclosed room . . . as many people as you can get on that door, you need to do that because you are going to experience this intense storm for a good while longer. Okay? It is not over, it's likely to get worse again."

Obviously upset, Madeline asked, "About how long?"

Norcross replied: "We have a long time to go. Okay? We have hours to go here before this is over. It's going to be very, very difficult, and you're just going to have to decide, 'We're going to stick together and we're going to make it through it.' Okay?"

Many people were living through an experience that was beyond frightening. Karen Baldwin found it "surreal":

We could hear the screen patio tearing away from the back of the house. We could actually hear the metal bending and ripping. . . . Attempting to open or close any interior door after four o'clock in the morning was incredibly difficult to do. . . . Probably the height of the storm hit us at five o'clock. I was scared. I've never been so scared in my life. I realized I was sitting in the room shaking. At least I thought I was shaking. And then I kind of took a deep breath and realized that it wasn't me shaking, it was the wall behind me that was literally moving back and forth, almost vibrating.

At that point, someone on the radio said if you don't feel secure where you are, you might want to seek an interior hallway in the house with no windows. So I announced this to Doug and Scott. . . . We no sooner got the door open, and the wind literally threw Scott across the room. As we went out, the living room door blew, at which point all three of the French doors in the back of the house broke. We literally crawled back to the bedroom, got the door closed again, pushed the dresser back up against the door, and were frantically trying to close the outside French doors into the bedroom. They had blown out, and we were holding onto the doors trying to hold them closed. It was impossible. Between the three of us we could not get them closed.

The storm continued. . . . I opened the bedroom door to check on the front doors. This was probably the height of stupidity for the evening. The whole force of the storm was coming through our front doors. I decided I had to close the front doors. So I went over to the doors and I tried to get the one door closed and I got it two-thirds closed. And I had to reach over to get the other door. So I am standing kind of almost spread-eagle in the doorway. And of course all the wind and rain and everything else was coming through the doors.

It was as if I was flying between the wind and the water. . . . The wind just took me and literally pushed me backward toward the wall in the dining room. It probably just pushed me about ten feet. . . . It was very surreal; the whole thing was surreal. I could see the doors, the wind, and the water coming in. And there I was, just slowly moving backwards with the force of the wind and the water.[10]

Retreating back to the bedroom, Karen rode out the rest of the storm with her husband and son. There was nothing the Baldwins could do, nothing many people in Dade County could do, as the homes that had been havens, safe retreats from the worries and threats of the outside world, were destroyed around them.

Faye McCloud, a counselor at Bowman Foster Ashe Elementary School, lived through the storm with her family in her house at 157th Street, about a mile east of Metrozoo. At first, like many other Miamians, she underestimated the potential strength of Hurricane Andrew. She had popped plenty of popcorn. She and her family had lots of candles. She thought they were going to be just fine, almost cozy.

I had woken up about 1:30 A.M. and cleaned up and vacuumed. We had a new aqua carpet, and I wanted to be prepared in case the electricity went off. About 4:30 my husband told me to look out of the window. I looked out and I was very frightened. I had never seen trees bend over like I saw them doing. I remember I told him that I was nervous. The sky had such an odd color and there was such tension around us. As if we knew that something was about to happen, we lit the candles.

My husband was attempting to put something over the windows when they blew. I grabbed the kids and ran to the garage that was attached to the house and put the kids in the car. My husband said,

"Faye, I have to go back in and blow out the candles." I said, "No, you can't go back in there. The hurricane is in the house." He said, "I need to go in and get the keys so we can move the car closer to the wall so the kitchen door won't bang open." I begged him not to go. Then he said, "I need to check on our neighbor who is by herself." I told him, "You cannot go! You cannot go! You just have to stay here!" Then we got in the second car that didn't have as much glass as the first.[11]

Like many people describing the hurricane at its worst, McCloud recalled "the horrible sound overhead—like a train. But as much as I was afraid, I didn't want to display that to the children. So we sang songs and named all of the people that we could think of that we know and said, "They're thinking of us". . . . We were so hot. . . . We just stayed there hearing all of the horrible sounds of things hitting the garage, not knowing what it was. We were terrified. We were afraid that the garage door would break open."[12]

Many in Dade County were unable to stay home and ride out the storm with their families. Margaret Sowell was on duty as a nurse at Deering Hospital the night of the storm. While she found it hard to be away from her family, she had confidence in her husband Bob's ability to take care of things at home. At the hospital the storm proved to be far worse than anyone anticipated. "During the storm all the windows broke. The winds got up real bad, and the windows were really rattling. So we decided to bring all the patients out into the hallway . . . and locked all the doors; . . . everybody really reacted well . . . nobody panicked. Well, one mother panicked, but other than that everyone was fine. We just told the mother who panicked that she wasn't helping her son any, that she needed to calm down."[13] About 4:00 A.M., the hospital lost its power. Half an hour later the hospital's emergency generator system blew up. Shortly afterward, the ceiling of the Psychiatric Unit collapsed and rain began to pour into the building. Patients and staff moved into the Intensive Care Unit, which was still intact.

For Sowell, the worst part of the storm came after the hospital roof collapsed. Despite the destruction, people remained remarkably calm and coped as best they could. Sowell recalled that her ward was completely dark.

All we had was the flashlight. There was no air-conditioning, no water, no lights, nothing. It was unreal. We were stepping over patients; . . . we were still using the toilet . . . what else could we do? And psych patients, as I said, were over beside us, too, and they were fantastic. I was absolutely amazed. You know, we had wondered if maybe they had premedicated the patients because of this. But they said no. Every single one of them was fantastic. And throughout this whole thing, . . . I wish you could have seen it, it was unbelievable: they had holes in the wall in the Intensive Care Unit, everything failed, and they were bagging [ventilating] patients for hours and hours and hours . . . the patients had been on ventilators. They had to do it manually. They sat there for hours just bagging these patients.[14]

As more and more windows gave way and the hospital's roof collapsed, water was pouring into the building. Sowell recalled that she was "sitting there singing 'Shall We Gather by the River' as all the water was pouring in. I said, 'Okay, let's have a song.' And after that I thought, 'I don't think this is the song I should be singing!'" Sowell found herself having to care for her patients and see to their needs, at the same time hoping that her family was all right. "I was really worried about my family because I knew how bad it was where we were, and I live just behind the hospital. So I was really thinking about my family."[15]

Edward T. Foote II was one of those who decided to ride out the storm in his home, despite the fact that he lived in an evacuation zone:

My wife and I were in our house. We were not supposed to be, because that was an evacuation zone, but we decided to stay, in part because that's our house, that's where we live, and we also decided that is was as safe as any place because it's up on a small ridge. The storm surge could not come up as high as the living space of the house . . . and also because it's a big old brick house and it did in fact survive the storm very well. . . .

We didn't sleep very much. We wandered around the house. The downstairs hallway was the only place where we could be away from the potential of exploding glass."

Foote and his wife, Roberta (Bosie), had little idea of what was going on around them. "For the first two or three hours, my wife and I were trying to understand what was happening to the house, and potentially to us. . . . The horrible sound of the wind and trees crashing against the house. . . . It was a very frightening experience. . . . That's what we did until dawn, then the winds began to subside. I was pleased to see we were still alive and that the house was still standing. Then, increasingly, I began to think about the university and how I would get there."[16]

Michael Tang, a Metro Dade police officer, was working throughout the storm.

We were basically in an Alpha Bravo shift, which is twelve hours on, twelve hours off, seven days a week. Basically we were on the road working until about an hour before the storm hit. . . . I was assigned to uniform duty—basically you are out on the road. We were assigned to our normal district, which is the Doral district. . . . It was ironic, because I thought that this was a really safe place to be [the Doral Country Club]—in fact, members of the squad were making jokes how we'd be the best treated there, because Doral is known for, you know, fancy service. Anyway, when the wind began to pick up and move trees around, our cars, too, it got too windy to drive, so we parked and ran into the hotel. . . . I thought it would be like the others—it would turn [out] like the other hurricanes did.

Driving to the hotel was crazy. The car started shaking real hard and you couldn't really go that fast because now you're really freaking out . . . trees are coming down and you could see cables slapping together and falling . . . the green glow of transformers blowing up. About that time, I began to wish I'd prepared better at my house, bought more to eat.

Once Tang got inside the Doral,

we could no longer hear the police radio, so I monitored Channel 7 and kept in tune with them, and basically got a really good view of it all. It was quite an experience and I lived to tell it, and it's something I'll never forget. . . . [I was] standing right in front of the main entrance, they've got big glass double doors. We were watching them, wondering which one was gonna go first, and if we would be fast enough to dodge it. We were just trying to face the situation with humor . . . we almost got a pool going to bet which door would blow in first and which person could best avoid it. We were joking, but it actually happened. I was standing next to them, talking on the phone with my mom, checking to see if everything was okay.

All of a sudden, I heard the wind really start to pick up . . . it was really strong and something just told me to turn around and when I turned around to look, I just dropped the phone and ran. The whole glass piece just fell in one piece and slapped the ground. Glass went everywhere. The whole Doral crew was there trying to close it up, everyone had come into the room, curious to see what was going on with all the screaming and running around. I was lucky to move because it would have fallen right on top of me. Once that happened, I was sure that there was gonna be a whole lot of damage out there, and it was serious.[17]

Lawrence Moose weathered the storm in Red Cross headquarters in the northwest section of town. He and other members of the organization stayed on the phones throughout the night—it went by him in a blur.

The information was changing so fast and the action was going so fast. It's hard to remember real details, but I remember, I think it must have been about two o'clock in the morning when I finally just passed out of exhaustion and I got a little bit of sleep, although I remember expecting at any time something to fly through the windows. . . .

We didn't have shuttering to begin with, and it was a problem because it had to be union made because it was [a] union building and we were having trouble getting that accomplished before the storm. So what we ended up doing was taking folding tables . . . took . . . the legs off the tables and bolted them up in front of the windows, so it really didn't help on the outside; . . . luckily none of the windows broke and nothing came flying through.[18]

Experiencing Andrew from Afar

The storm was a terrifying experience not just for those who lived through it in Dade County, but also for their family members and friends who happened to be elsewhere in the country. Cristina Quintairos, a medical student at Georgetown University, described calling her family from Arlington, Virginia. "I called my house, and I was talking to my sister, and she was telling me that the wind was howling, and that a lot of things were flying and hitting walls and the windows of the house. And she told me that the sliding doors and windows were vibrating. . . . All at once, she heard a loud noise in the back of the house, but it was too dark to see what had actually happened. . . . Throughout this whole time, she was hearing transformers blowing, and seeing the lights flashing from the transformers. She said this was the only source of light during the hurricane." Quintarios found the experience extremely unsettling. "I was already picturing the destruction that could occur in Miami—just picturing, like, the familiar sites just being destroyed. At that time, I already knew if something serious happened to my family, I would return home and help out, because I felt it wouldn't be right for me to be here, living the good life when everybody at home was either hurt or despaired."[19]

Irene Baljet remained stranded in Atlanta, unable to do anything to help her family.

My husband has been heavily trained in the military, so I wasn't upset about him. I knew he wouldn't panic. I knew he would know what to do. I was totally at ease in regards to my husband, even though I would have liked to be there. I was more concerned with her [her daughter] because I've always been the provider of—What's the word for it?—the softer side in the family. My husband is the rock. I've always been the one they come to when they're feeling sad, when they need to talk about something that is bothering them.

Exactly as I thought [it] would, it happened. He secured the house, secured the roof and everything that could be secured by himself, worked for fourteen hours without even eating, and then went to bed. So my daughter was awake all night, listening to the wind, scared to death. . . . She was in essence by herself through this, and that was my concern. I knew it would happen. My husband is very practical and he was of course exhausted and he would say, "Hey, there is nothing I can do."

Baljet had talked to her daughter more than once on Sunday as the storm was approaching Miami.

I had spoken to my daughter several times because I was also very worried about my kitty cat. She is an outside cat. . . . They couldn't find her. They finally found her, and the last time I talked to her [her daughter] was at 10:00 or 10:30 at night. The cat was in, the house was tied down. I said, "Okay, call me as soon as the storm is over because I need to know that you are okay. . . ."

The [airline flight] crew stayed up until about midnight talking about the storm and what was going to happen, how we were going to get home, because we anticipated the airport closing and not being able to get home the next day. Finally at midnight, we all said our goodnights, went to our rooms, and I watched the weather channel and CNN. . . . I had the weather channel on one and CNN on the other. I was going back and forth until about 1:00 A.M.. At that time I thought, "This is silly, there is nothing I can do except torture myself," so I turned it off and went to sleep. . . .

Interestingly enough at 5:14 A.M. exactly, I woke up for no reason and immediately put the TV on, and at that time, the TV station was being [gutted by the storm]. . . . The manager had stayed up until the very last minute. The windows were broken, the wind was coming in, and the man outside was saying, "We're leaving. This has become hazardous." So they were completing their transmission, closing down. . . . In all of this without knowing if your family is all right.[20]

Saying Good-Byes

Across the southern part of Dade County, where roofs were ripping off, windows breaking, and doors flying open, all you could hear were things crashing about, metal scraping, and the roaring wind. Children watched as their houses "broke" and pleaded with their parents to call 911. Some people began saying their good-byes.

Alexis Martinez slept through the first part of the hurricane. At about four in the morning he was awakened by a shattering sound, at which point the electricity went out throughout his house. As the storm progressed, many thoughts went through his mind: "I was scared for myself, my family. I was scared for my friends. . . . I needed to know how some friends were [doing], that were in houses that were not as strong as mine. . . . I was concerned about just pretty much keeping calm myself. . . . I tried to keep in touch with everybody. I called friends. I called family members. Luckily, the phone was intact. Nothing happened to the telephone lines, so we were able to keep in touch with everybody."[21]

Sharon Johnson, a professor at Miami-Dade Community College, said that "the shaking was just unbelievable." Sharon, her husband, mother-in-law, and Labrador retriever weathered Andrew in a closet. They could feel the force of wind blowing through the house and hear the explosions and pops as the windows went. They knew that there had to be quite a bit of damage to the house. "Then to hear on the radio that the eye was now approaching; . . . I don't think the house could have taken much more. . . . We figured that we were in real trouble at that point . . . of course, the whole time I kept thinking to myself, 'They told me to leave. Why didn't I leave? . . . They're going to find me dead and they're going to say, "Ah, now here is another one of these stupid people that was told to leave and didn't.""" The Johnsons remained calm, however. "We were very quiet," Sharon recalls, but "at one point we held hands and prayed. We thought we were in big trouble."[22]

Art Carlson, a lifetime resident of Miami, had spent the hours before the storm reporting for Channel 10 TV on preparations in Broward County. Despite this assignment, he was able to be with his wife and their two children in Coconut Grove during the storm.

I was on the ground floor of our home on Royal Palm Avenue. We had pulled mattresses off the beds in the children's rooms, and we were all huddled in the hallway between the kitchen and the bedrooms. With all the dogs, five dogs. It was not my idea of a fun evening, but that's where we were. . . . My biggest concern was trying to keep my wife and children calm and not panicked, because, you know, I knew that there wasn't much that we could do about it. We were on the high rock ridge there, fourteen feet above sea level, and I didn't think, under the worst of conditions with the storm surge, we'd get nailed. But I was concerned about flying debris and things like that.

If I got up and walked around the house once, I did it a hundred times during the storm, because every time something would make a noise my wife would go, "What was that?" and I'd have to go and check. We had one leak during the storm, and that was it. . . .

The wind howling through the various shutters on the doors and the windows and all made an incredible noise. About four o'clock in the morning in pitch blackness, I was laying there, and all of a sudden I felt a little hand on my shoulder, and it was my seven year old, Cameron, and he just said very calmly and quietly, "Daddy, I'm scared." And I reached out and I pulled him over to me and I said, "Cameron, we're all scared, but we're going to be okay, you know, we're doing fine." It wasn't until days later that I realized, looking at some color radar maps, that we had sustained, here in the Grove [Coconut Grove], winds of 150 miles per hour for the hour or two that it went over us. So I probably should have been more concerned than I was, but I wasn't.[23]

Ross McGill Jr., executive director of the Boy Scouts of America for Dade County, found the storm an equally frightening experience: "It was terrifying. For three and one-half hours we huddled in this walk-in closet with a mattress between us and the door, and I have two cats and we had our cats in there in a cage. . . . The house shook. It sounded like a train coming through our house. When I say [it] shook, it literally shook. I thought the house would fly any minute, and I was really terrified." Despite his fear, McGill felt that he was fortunate to be surviving. "I thought about how lucky I was. I thought about the fact that every minute I was still there, . . . I wasn't gone. I was thinking, I was very prayerful, I was very thankful that I had my wife with me. . . . It just didn't dawn on me that I could really die, even though I was terrified."[24]

For many, the fury of the storm led them to reflect on their loved ones and whether they would live to see them again. James White had left his apartment on Miami Beach and was weathering out the storm with friends in Coral Gables. Huddled inside a bathroom with four other people and listening to updates on the storm on the radio, he asked himself: "Will I see my mother again? I just left her. I hadn't seen her in eight years. What is she thinking about? What are my daughters thinking about? I'm sure they're keeping up with Hurricane Andrew."[25]

For Pat Ashley, one of the pastors at Pinecrest Presbyterian Church, the storm provided an opportunity for reflection and spiritual growth:

> I was in my apartment. . . . Alone. It was certainly my choice and I have no regrets about that. I found it a time of real self-discovery and prayer. . . . I was very aware of feeling safe—not necessarily physically safe. Although it really didn't occur to me that I would be injured or die. It occurred to me later when I saw what the storm had done. But there was a sense of power—a sense of danger, but also a sense of my own larger safety in it, that whatever happened there was a larger "okayness" about whatever happened that comes out of God's care for me.
>
> I was aware of being very grateful for the radio and just imagining living in a time when there was no warning for such a storm, or much less warning, and no communication during it. My gratitude was for the statement, "Here it is now, here's the time frame we're looking at." For somebody to be in the middle of it and not have any idea when it might be over—I found myself really imagining what it would have been like without the resources that we have. Sort of aware of that vulnerability and glad for the contact with the outside world. Especially, of course, for the way Bryan Norcross was.[26]

Bryan Norcross: The Guide Through the Storm

In disasters such as Hurricane Andrew, unexpected heroes often emerge. Perhaps during Andrew no one touched as many people as WTVJ-Channel 4 weatherman Bryan Norcross. Throughout the interviews for this work, Norcross's name came up time and time again. After the storm, Norcross received hundreds of calls and letters of appreciation, as well as three marriage proposals. In South Dade, one family wrote, "Thank you Bryan Norcross" across their roof, while a banner at Southwest 131st Street and 145th Avenue declared "Bryan Norcross for President."[27]

Much of Norcross's effectiveness resulted from his recognition that the storm was a sociological, as well as a meteorological, phenomenon. As he explained: "Once the storm is bearing down on you it becomes a sociological issue. How does a society respond to the crisis. . . . If you looked at the overall scope of the coverage immediately around the crisis, it was about 15 percent meteorology and 85 percent social assistance, in terms of evacuation and shelters and electricity." According to Norcross, providing information that would help people cope with the storm was problematic for most of the other television stations in town. The approach taken at Norcross's station was not only to report on the hurricane, but also to help people cope and deal with the effects of the storm.

> The fact is that in the other television stations they did not know about what to say, and they didn't have any place to get the information, because the television news departments, in general, are set up to respond to an event. It's really an event-driven kind of process where something happens. The television reporter goes out and either observes it or asks about it and dutifully reports what they saw or what they are told. . . . This was an entirely different mechanism. What we were asked to do, or what we did, and what the other stations were unable to do two days prior to the storm, was anticipate what was going to happen.[28]

Norcross and his colleagues didn't simply track the storm, they told people what to anticipate and how to prepare.

Norcross and his producer Scott Seavers had spent a great deal of time asking questions about problems that might come up in a hurricane emergency situation; they found the answers by running tests and by talking to experts. "The issue, for instance, of do you leave a window open?" Norcross explained. "We asked I don't know how many structural engineers and wind research people the specific question, because that question has come up so often. . . . Do I really have to evacuate? So what's the law? What's the procedure going to be? Are they going to come and drag me out if I don't go?" Their preparation made it possible for Norcross to talk people through the storm.

> The phone calls turned out to be vital in just allowing people—and I had this told to me over and over again—that felt so alone, that they felt that they were the only ones going through it ("It couldn't possibly be this bad for everybody else."), to find it was this bad for other people, and that made it much more bearable for them to realize that other people were going through the same thing, and that when I said to Madeline Martinez, "You've got to hold that door!" that inspired other people to get up and hold the door because other people were going through the same situation. That is what turned out to be so critical.[29]

Sharon Johnson and her family were also listening to Norcross. He gave them a "sense of what was going on" that was very important, she recalls, although "it wasn't always totally accurate, in terms of where the storm was; . . . there we are in the closet . . . people are calling in . . . from Kendall . . . [Norcross] says, 'Okay, people, now, down in Perrine, Cutler Ridge, we're not hearing anybody. Gosh, must not be anything going on. How come you guys aren't calling?' [Laughter] No, that's not the reason why we're not calling. We're in major trouble down here."[30]

Through his calm voice and his commonsense suggestions, Norcross created a shared experience for many members of the community. In fact, more than any other recent event, Hurricane Andrew bound the people of South Florida together. We all—rich and poor, young and old, healthy and infirm—experienced the storm's terror. Andrew did not discriminate. We all had no choice but to try to live through it. Only afterward, when it was safe to come out, did we begin to discover that for some of us, Norcross was right—it had been very, very bad.

Coming Out after the Storm

3

As Hurricane Andrew roared across the Everglades, it left 275 small planes at the Kendall-Tamiami Airport damaged beyond repair, tossed about like toys. On Key Biscayne, 325 acres of Australian pines were leveled in Bill Baggs State Park. Powerboats were stacked on top of each other in Sailboat Bay in Coconut Grove or marooned in yards and streets, hundreds of feet from the water. Trees, power lines, and traffic lights were down everywhere. Hurricane Andrew had killed thirteen people.

An ocean-going tugboat left high and dry by the storm surge. (Image ID: wea00530)

Immediately following the storm no one understood the enormity of what had happened. Some radio and television anchors and reporters, like Bryan Norcross, suspected, however, that it was very bad because of the phone calls they had been receiving during the night. By 7:00 or 7:30 A.M. Monday, August 24, it was clear that the worst was over. People all over Dade County began to realize that South Florida would never be the same.

Coming Out

Coming out of their safe places inside their houses and out of their houses into their neighborhoods, especially in the southern part of the county, people faced unprecedented levels of destruction. Michael Laughlin said that after the storm he and his family "walked into the living room and noticed that the family room and the kitchen was missing the roof completely. The trusses were up there, but the roof and the drywall ceiling collapsed. About half of the living room was missing wood and ceiling. . . . I walked around the backyard and I noticed that the neighborhood looked like it was when we first bought the house. . . . All the fences were gone. The bushes were gone, all the hedges, swing sets—everything was gone. It was just like someone had dropped a bomb in our vicinity. . . . It was just flat."[1]

Sharon Johnson and her family "didn't quite know when it was over." They were thinking about leaving their closet when "we heard our neighbors . . . shouting . . . and then we came out." They discovered that their screened porch was ripped off. In the living room "everything was just glass and rubble, everything was soaking wet . . . all the windows had been blown out." Then they walked out front to find that "our garage door had blown in . . . porch lights torn off . . . ; people . . . just walked around [to] see what the rest of the neighborhood looked like . . . was everybody okay? People were cut up . . . everybody had stories."[2]

Once they were sure that the storm was over, Faye McCloud's husband left the family in their car in the garage and went back into their house alone: "When he came back, he was crying. He said, 'Faye, I just can't believe it. Our house is gone.' I could not even believe what he was telling me. I couldn't comprehend what he was saying. So I went inside, and he stayed in the car with the kids. I could not believe it. It was just beyond anything that you might see in a theater—in a good movie where you feel that you are there. Except, I was really there. I was so stunned, and so shocked and so hurt."[3]

In Miami Lakes, Ross McGill came out of the closet he and his wife had huddled in throughout the storm to find three rooms in his house totally destroyed. There was major water damage throughout the entire structure, and a third of his roof was gone. "After the storm we came out, like six o'clock the next morning, and I was walking around my house in four or five inches of water, furniture wet and carpets sopping, and glass and debris everywhere . . . every tree totally down and just demolished." When he went outdoors, McGill said, "I had lost my roof and [I was] looking at the damage in the neighborhood and assessing the damage, and that's when I truly realized that we were very, very lucky. I had my life and my wife—the two things that matter. I had been spared . . . I wasn't homeless." While considering himself fortunate, McGill nonetheless felt that the impact of the storm on him was devastating: "We lost a little better than a third of our home. Our roof, which was a gravel roof, was gone down to the wood. We lost windows. Three rooms were just trashed; . . . we had to rebuild totally, and then we had water throughout the house, major water damage. It took all of my patio, just took it away."[4]

James White, who had evacuated from Miami Beach and weathered the storm with friends in Coral Gables, said that the destruction caused by Andrew reminded him of a battle zone.

> Right after the hurricane passed we weren't sure whether or not we should open the door and look out. Part of that was fear of not knowing what to expect and whether or not, in fact, the hurricane was over, even though the radio had indicated that it had passed. . . . Eventually, we opened the door and [it was] just a total shock. . . . I just couldn't believe the damage . . . trees were down. . . . It . . . just looked like a catastrophe and . . . we walked out; . . . neighbors of course were also out and people were checking on one another's homes and seeing if everyone was okay and there were some cars turned over. . . . It just looked like a battle zone.[5]

Grace Laskis discovered "devastation everywhere . . . the family room was in the kitchen. . . . Glass, water, everywhere and the plywood was in the yard. . . . But we found one of our cats in the garbage can, and one was in a closet—my daughters were so happy. . . . Neighbors came out in a daze . . . amazed that they were still alive . . . going in the middle of the street to see what their houses looked like. . . . They couldn't understand why the one place they stayed in had made it. . . . One girl had used a mattress as protection but glass had cut through it and she was cut up pretty bad."[6]

The Baldwins didn't venture out until about 7:30 A.M.. They realized that it was still raining and the wind was still blowing, so they "just kind of stuck around the house until the wind and rain died down enough that we could get out and see what had happened. Karen remembers walking around,

> picking things that are soaking wet up off the floor . . . just to pick something up and look at it and wring it out and hang it over a chair or a table . . . even walking around and going, "Gee, all of our porch furniture was inside wasn't it?" . . . You're standing there and count-ing chairs and pieces of porch furniture . . . and then realizing that some of the furniture that had been in the house was now residing in the swimming pool in the back yard. . . . When the front doors blew, our refrigerator was blown out from the wall. The door was flung open from the refrigerator, and a good portion of the food was liter-ally blown into the swimming pool. I can remember coming out and looking at the refrigerator to see what food remained, but at that point the darn refrigerator had been standing open with no electricity for several hours, and I'm standing there saying, "Oh, we can save this bottle of ketchup. . . ."
>
> Weird things go through your mind. . . . I had a little glass container of potpourri . . . that had a brass top on it . . . that was on a table in the living room; . . . the table was just splintered, it was a wicker table, it was in pieces on the floor. The brass top was right next to it on the floor. . . . I picked it up, and of course it's wet, so you're drying it off and finding a dry place to lay it down. . . . I walked to the pool and here's the bottle of the darn potpourri container that's glass, with the

potpourri still in it, as dry as can be, the glass is intact, and [I] brought it back inside. . . .

The whole thing was *not real*. It was like a surrealistic movie or a painting. Ah, it was almost like you were there and you weren't there.

Karen guessed that it was around 2:00 P.M. when she and her family finally ventured outside. She recalls that it was

bizarre . . . to the sense that, ah, it was not so much "Oh, wow, look at all the damage to the house" or "How are we ever going to get out of it?" It wasn't like that at all. It was more like, "Wow, look at that, look at those trees that are down! This is totally awesome". . . . Almost like watching it in a movie. This is something that you look at and it's going to go away . . . and it wasn't until much later . . . the idea that it wasn't going to go away and you had to deal with it on a minute-to-minute and hour-to-hour basis. But right then, it was more, kind of, fascination, excitement almost, of looking at it and seeing exactly what had happened.[7]

Checking on the Neighborhood

Overnight, Hurricane Andrew had forever altered familiar surroundings and cherished rituals. Peter Schulz, an undergraduate student at the University of Miami, recalled how after getting a few hours of sleep, he rode his bicycle from his dormitory at the university to Coconut Grove. What he saw as he rode toward the bay was "like nothing I had ever seen in my life. Everything was in upheaval. Unbelievable. People were all out in the streets with, like, no clue what to do. In the Grove it was unreal. We saw people ransacking stores and taking all sorts of stuff. . . . The boats were crazy. There were boats in the middle of the road alongside the bay in the Grove . . . just sitting there, like they belonged or something, but they were totally ruined."[8] The tidal surge that brought those large boats up into the streets of Coconut Grove also caused extensive damage to homes, such as those in L'Hermitage Villas, an exclusive condominium in the Grove. At least a foot and a half of water was still standing on the grounds at 9:00 A.M. Monday morning. Almost 75 percent of the villas at L'Hermitage lost everything on their first floors, which were under four and a half feet of water.

Even though Mike Puller had put his boat sideways in its slip on Key Biscayne, he discovered after the storm that "two of the heavy ropes broke during the storm, and we took some damage on one side of the boat. The outriggers were totally bent over sideways, so we had to get new ones. And the whole dock was stripped of all the boxes, and cutting tables were torn out." Following the storm, debris from Puller's dock was found over a mile away on Virginia Key.[9]

After Andrew, television anchor Art Carlson experienced a Miami he had never seen before. Trapped in his neighborhood by fallen trees, Carlson was unable to drive out in order to get to the television station.

There were trees down, not only blocking our driveway and blocking all our cars in, but there were enough trees down in the neighborhood that you couldn't go more than a block in any direction before you ran into a massive tree over the road. So I said, "If somebody wants me at the station, then they're going to have to come and get me. I mean, that's a fact of life." So they said, "Okay, we'll send somebody down." They got down here about two hours later, and there was so much destruction with trees down in the Grove that I had to hike out six blocks. That was as close as you could get to the house—which made for an interesting couple of days after the storm. . . .

It took a week to get all the trees off the road down the major arteries, so I could get out. The result of that was that somebody had to come get me every morning at 4:15 in the morning. And so here I was, working the daybreak shift, hiking out of the neighborhood in utter pitch blackness, because [there was] no power anywhere. With just a flashlight, [I was] climbing over trees, walking around paths that had kind of been formed informally through the neighborhood, hiking out those six blocks, and waiting on a bus bench for a photographer to come down to the point that I could get out and we could go back to work.

That was very interesting. I have never, in all my life—I'm a native Miamian, and a native Grovite for that matter—and I have never in all my years experienced a stillness or an inky blackness like there was the first couple of days afterward. The stillness was unbelievable. It sounded to me like the third battalion rolling through the neighborhood with just me walking across through the leaves and over the branches. I was the only noise that you could hear . . . no birds, no crickets, no nothing, just absolutely still.[10]

Until power was restored throughout the county, it was strangely quiet throughout the night and early morning hours. The air was extraordinarily clear because the hurricane had blown away all of the dust. But once the sun came up, trees that were down or had lost all their leaves no longer provided shade, and South Florida became unbearably hot and harsh. The quiet disappeared with the unrelenting whine of chain saws and the constant sound of helicopters flying overhead.

Barren trees and unrelenting sunlight contributed to the sense of living in a blast zone. This was especially true in Dade County's more southern neighborhoods such as South Kendall, Cutler Ridge, Goulds, Perrine, Naranja, Leisure City, Homestead, and Florida City, where the storm had let loose its main fury. In these communities the destruction was most often described as being like the blast zone of an atomic bomb, or like carpet bombing in Vietnam. Dan Piet, who lived in Delray Beach, had come down to South Miami to clean up the property of a friend who was in Paris. As he traveled around after the storm, Piet said: "The extent of the damage I've seen is horrendous. The further south I go, as far south as Homestead, it looks like an atomic bomb hit it."[11]

I. J. Hudson, a reporter with WRC-TV in Washington, D.C., who was sent to South Florida immediately after the hurricane to report on the disaster for NBC News, described seeing widespread devastation beyond anything he could possibly imagine.

I've been in Vietnam. I've seen a lot of tornadoes that have done a lot of nasty stuff. And the best way that I've been able to describe it [Hurricane Andrew] to colleagues is that if this happened to one house in their entire viewing area, if that amount of devastation happened to one house, you'd have a live truck and another crew out there. It would be horrible—a major-league story. Well, it happened to 180,000 houses. And when you get that idea—that there's nothing above your eye level in many instances—that's how major it is. But still, until someone actually gets here and stands in the middle of it and feels it . . . it doesn't mean anything."

According to Hudson, the experience of the aftermath of the storm in South Dade was like the first time you go to a murder scene "where the body has been there several days. You don't see the body at first. All of a sudden, all of these senses come into play and you get a really good feeling for what people are actually living through."[12]

Because of the demands of his anchor job at the television station, Art Carlson was not able to drive down to the southern half of the county to see the damage until three weeks after Andrew struck.

When I got down there, I was dumbfounded. I mean, even three weeks after the storm, I was dumbfounded at the scope and the magnitude of the destruction. And nobody really did comprehend it. I mean, the storm came in on early Monday morning, and nobody really comprehended what the storm was until late Tuesday, until you got up in a helicopter and were able to really look. And then it was just like, yeah, there's a lot of damage, and then the damage never ended—as far as you could see, it never ended.

The thing that I was struck by, three weeks afterwards, driving down through it—going down the turnpike at about 152nd Street and south, looking east toward the bay—I was struck by the fact that I could see every roof in every neighborhood. There were no trees, none to be seen at all. Obviously the scope of the destruction of the houses and all that, . . . and within a couple of days after that I remember driving back up from Homestead one day, and the scene just sticks in my mind indelibly. Coming up on the turnpike there in Florida City, just getting on, heading north, to the right [I could see] scores upon scores of damaged town homes, just laying in ruins. To the left—and this was all at once, you could see it all at once—damaged town homes on the right, tent cities going up on the left, helicopters absolutely everywhere, and large transports flying in and out of Homestead Air Force Base, which you could now see, when you could never see it before. By that time they had already started burning a lot of the trash, and so you had these great plumes of smoke coming up all over the place, which made it look like something out of the old film *The Day After*. I mean, it was just holocaust, it was unbelievable.[13]

Not everyone was able to get out to survey the damage to their neighborhoods immediately following the storm. At Deering Hospital, once the storm had subsided, Margaret Sowell had to "try and get some drinks for the patients because there was no food. They had gone the whole day without food. Nobody had any food. . . . I went down to get at least some juice for the patients. The water was pouring down in the kitchen, too. The ceiling was sagging real bad. . . . I took some juice up to the patients—at least they had some juice. Nobody complained. Not one single person said, 'I'm hungry. You didn't feed me.' It was unreal. It was fantastic." Sowell went on to describe the patients' evacuation:

> Before the hurricane, they had transferred or evacuated patients from Miami Beach Community Hospital to our hospital because they thought Miami Beach Hospital would be hit bad. As it turned out, we had all these evacuated patients at Deering, and Miami Beach wasn't touched. So then in the morning after everything calmed down we had to evacuate all those patients back [to Miami Beach] as well as ours. . . . We had to carry them downstairs. Nothing worked. It was unreal.
>
> We got real close. We had to go in the medication room and use the bedpans ourselves. Everybody did. People had to use bedpans in the hallway. We tried to cover them best we could with a towel for privacy. It was unreal. The thing was, we couldn't get to the clean water or the dirty water because it was locked in one of the rooms.

Transporting the patients from Deering Hospital back to Miami Beach took Sowell and the other members of the staff the entire day. It was not until early Monday evening that she finally got to return home. She had been dropped off at work the previous day by her husband and got a ride home with one of the other nurses on her floor.

> When we went out to get in her car—a brand-new 1993 car, she had it two weeks—it was demolished. This was Linda, the other RN that had worked with me. So she took me—her car was still driveable. . . . We couldn't go through any of the back roads because everything

was blocked off, so we had to go out to US 1, go out to 144th Street and then backtrack. But everything was on the road—electrical wires, water, and everything—and we were really scared because we thought, "Well, we survived the hurricane and everything just to be electrocuted." It took us about an hour to drive what would be a five-minute drive. . . . I mean, we had to go out and move some bushes and branches off the road. It was just horrendous. There were trees down everywhere. Of course, the house, it was—I mean, Bob and the kids, they had cleaned it up, but it was still terrible. It was awful.[14]

Sowell's house had received some water damage inside, but she considered herself far better off than many others around her. During the next few days, she and her husband helped others in their neighborhood get their homes and yards back in order.

Reaching Out to One Another

People coming out of their damaged homes to view their neighborhoods frequently found themselves thrust into emergency rescue operations. Mike Brescher weathered Hurricane Andrew in his house in Homestead with his wife, his mother, two dogs, and three cats. When he checked on the condominiums down the street after the storm, he realized that an elderly couple who lived in one of the units was probably trapped inside.

I saw that they had parked their car down the street a ways. So I knew they were in the condo somewhere. So we started digging through the rubble, because their house was totaled. They were in the bathroom. The whole thing had collapsed in on them. We worked to get them out. They were in their nightclothes. He had caught a 2 X 4 right on the knuckles and it had ripped back the skin about five or six inches. . . . He had three broken ribs and a dislocated shoulder. I had to get him out. . . . She had a dislocated hip or something, and they were in shock.

The bad part was there was all this insulation. You know, the pink stuff they sell. . . . This stuff was like crust. It just painted these peoples' faces. And all the tar from the roofs, it just went into the air and these people had it embedded in their faces and eyes and ears.[15]

Brescher and his neighbors ended up rescuing several other people in the neighborhood. Eventually, police and paramedic services arrived to help them.

People who were involved in coordinating rescue efforts, like Lawrence Moose, who was at Red Cross headquarters, had no opportunity to go out and survey the damage from the storm. As Moose recalled:

> It was still dark when we started working. The first thing that we tried to do was get in touch with the shelters immediately to see how they were and if there were any problems there—their staffing needs, their food needs, if they knew of anyone who was injured, if there were any problems at all in the shelters. That was my primary concern, and then getting supplies to them and getting food to them was my second concern right away. . . . We had a big bottleneck [with] the phone lines. . . . We were getting calls from . . . about fifty different shelters . . . all over the building, and the building is so big we were running from one table to another to try to get in touch with these shelter managers.

Outside help arrived at Red Cross headquarters by the middle of Monday afternoon.

> At 3:00 P.M. or so in the afternoon some people came in from . . . Orlando . . . where they were prestaging some supplies and people. . . . We hadn't slept very much (and we hadn't eaten very well, even)— just a couple of hours since Saturday—and they were staying at a nearby hotel, and they let me go take thirty minutes off to get a shower and come right back. And it wasn't until then when I actually went out into the area that I realized that just in this area around the airport there were so many trees down and so many roads blocked, and of course, no one had power. . . . My first thoughts were, "What am I going to do with these shelters to get them food."

Later in the week Moose made it down to the southern end of the county to survey the extent of the damage. Only then did the enormity of what had occurred fully hit him. "I didn't really understand it until a couple of days later when I actually got down there. . . . I got off on Eureka Drive, which is where I always used to get off when I lived down there, and drove into an area which I used to live. . . . You really can't say anything. Tears just started coming to my eyes, because it was just so different than it had been three or four days earlier. There was really nothing to say. It was just overwhelming when I saw it."[16]

Amid all the confusion, people began to reach out to one another in new ways. "Neighbors that we'd never spoken to before," Grace Laskis said, "now we were asking, 'How are you?' We became very personal."[17] New relationships and new ways of interacting with others in the neighborhoods and throughout the community were already beginning to emerge.

Returning Home

For those who had weathered Andrew at a friend's house or in a shelter, returning home was usually a traumatic experience. Pat Warren, who lived off Howard Drive, east of US 1, had spent the night of the storm at the Baptist Hospital rehab center with her disabled son. When she left the hospital on Kendall Drive and headed east toward Dixie Highway: "I saw everything all over the road. And when I saw the church—the Baptist church—with half of it gone . . . when I came from the expressway, I couldn't believe it, and then it was like a war zone. . . . When I saw my house and all the screening in the pool, the windows gone, the roof gone, . . . I was devastated. I just thought, there was no way I'm going to come out of this. No way I'm going to come out of it."[18]

It took Paul Dee two hours to work his way through the debris back to his neighborhood on Monday morning—normally a ten- to twelve-minute drive. Dee said he felt like a "rat, and they had changed the maze on me." Finally, he had to leave his car about three blocks from his house "and walk the rest of the way because the road was impassable. The first thing that I saw was cars in the driveway, which was odd, since I left them in the garage. It was at that point that I knew we had suffered a devastating loss. Whatever force had moved the two automobiles had certainly moved everything else." Dee's house, which was located next to the Deering Bay golf course, had metal storm shutters on all of its windows. The storm surge from the hurricane, however, had bent them apart, allowing an eight-foot wall of water to surge through his home. After making a survey of the damage, he went to see if he could find any of his neighbors. "No one was there. I returned to my house and walked through it. It was a foot deep in bay-bottom mud and debris, which was left behind when the water receded. The furnishings of the house had been totally destroyed. On top of what remained of the inside of my home was debris from the marina a block down from the house. Gas tanks, boat motors, pilings were actually lying over my furniture."[19] After going through the rest of his house, Dee realized that most of his furniture was missing and must have been swept away in the tidal surge. He eventually found a few heavily damaged pieces of furniture several blocks from the house. A buffet with china still sitting in it made its way across the street and onto the golf course without a single dish or saucer being damaged.

Although Roberta Smith lived in a trailer in Richmond Heights, she had decided to weather the storm in a motel room near Miami International Airport. Once the storm was over, after checking on her sister in Richmond Heights, she went to see if her trailer had survived Hurricane Andrew. "Nothing was there . . . there was nothing. . . . Nothing! I didn't know what to do. . . . There was nothing left . . . everything was gone. . . . Everything that I ever owned was in the trailer. Everything."[20] Despite the destruction of her home and everything that she owned, Smith considered herself fortunate to have her health and to be alive. She was thankful that her family had come through the storm without serious injury.

Irene Baljet, still stranded in Atlanta with the other members of her flight crew, received a call from her daughter at 8:00 A.M. on Monday morning. Her daughter said,

"Mom, this is terrible". . . . Of course, my next question was, "Is everyone okay?" She said, "Yes." My next question was, "Is the house okay?" She said, "Yes, but everything is gone in the neighborhood." She was shaken. So I asked her to put her father on the telephone. He's the coolest cucumber, this man, but I could hear an edge to his voice that I have never heard, and we have been through a lot together in twenty-six years. . . . When I asked . . . a silly question . . . about some of my trees . . . finally he said to me, "Irene, it's total devastation around here."

Baljet met with the other members of her flight crew at breakfast. "We had a little meeting as to how we were going to get home because the airport was closed. We had heard that American had lost the Ionosphere Club. We had seen an airplane at the airport all broken up with the nose down. . . . I kept saying to them, 'Something is wrong, something is very wrong in Miami, there is something about the way [my husband] is saying, "We're fine, we're fine,"' but I could hear other than that."[21]

Baljet and her crew assumed that flying back on Monday was out of the question. On Tuesday, they were told that the airport in Miami was still closed and that all of the flights through Ft. Lauderdale were completely booked. At that point, according to Baljet: "The crew decided we would rent a van and drive down to Miami. . . . They thought we were maybe six hours from Miami. I told them, 'You're eleven hours''. . . . The captain said, 'Okay, tomorrow is Wednesday. If we do not get priority passes and Miami doesn't open, I'm renting a car. Whoever wants to join me, I will drive for eleven hours or whatever it takes. . . .' Luckily, the next morning when we got up, we heard that the company was bringing us through Miami airport and we had priority passes, so we would get on. But of course all this time we were watching CNN and watching Homestead."[22]

While in Atlanta, Baljet saw pictures of her husband's destroyed office on Cable News Network. As she recalled, it was "one of the most damaged buildings in the Dadeland Center. Here I'm looking, this is our livelihood . . . and there are no windows left. . . . I'm just going berserk." As she saw pictures of Homestead and Florida City, she described it as "really strange. It was like you were seeing a movie. You keep thinking, 'That can't be!'"[23]

Baljet was finally able to fly back to Miami on Wednesday. Remembering that she had parked her car under a tree in the airport parking lot, she was worried about whether or not it had fallen on her car. Instead,

the tree fell in the other direction, so it didn't damage my car. . . . But Wednesday, when I drove into our neighborhood . . . all this time I had wanted to cry when I saw the pictures on TV . . . so I had not allowed myself to cry, but this complete devastation; . . . by this time my phones didn't work, so I couldn't communicate with my family. . . . So I'm driving towards my neighborhood, and as I'm driving south on the Palmetto, it is getting worse and worse progressively, and the knot in my throat is getting higher and higher. . . . I drove through Sunset. . . . I could not believe my eyes because there were trees that were maybe a yard, yard and a half, in diameter through the trunk, and they were down. Then I came down 87th and the sidewalks were uprooted by the trees when they fell. . . .

By now I'm getting close to home and beginning to get a knot in my stomach that says, "Do I really have a house standing? Did they tell me not to worry because there was nothing I could do. . . ?" I'm beginning to really get fearful and anxious. When I got to Kendall and 97th, I was stopped by the National Guard and they asked for my driver's license. I lost it completely! I was not crying, I was bawling! The poor soldier was looking at me, and I'm fumbling through my bag and I can't find my driver's license, so I finally, in sheer frustration, handed her my airline ID card, which has no address on it. It really didn't serve the purpose, but I think she realized that I was in such bad shape at that moment that she just waved me on.

Baljet arrived at a scene of total devastation.

We had what I felt was a very beautiful yard and suddenly I felt, my God, it looks like Connecticut in the winter. There was not a single leaf on anything. Everything was brown—parching heat. Wednesday was one of the hottest days . . . no rain. . . . Everything was absolutely brown like you never see in Florida. You never see that landscape. Everything was down. It was like a ghost town. My husband came out, and of course, I just lost it again. I could not believe what had happened. By this time he had . . . started cleaning up and started to salvage some things in the yard.[24]

Alicia Jeffers, who had evacuated from the area and spent the night of the hurricane in a hotel in Orlando with her husband, Lennox, and their daughter, had watched the progress of the storm on CNN. Having great difficulty sleeping, she and her husband "woke up in the morning, and we [turned on the TV]. It was hard to find any news. Finally something came on CNN, and it showed Cutler Ridge Mall. I thought, 'Oh, my God,' and I'm about fifteen minutes north of Cutler Ridge. And it kept talking about Homestead, and the only thing close to our home they talked about was Cutler Ridge Mall. It was pretty bad." Late on Monday night Jeffers and her husband were able to contact her husband's office manager. "She had friends staying with her during the storm that lived near us . . . she said that it was very bad, that they went back home to a shell. And that was when we realized that we were in deep trouble. That more than likely we had damage—severe damage."[25]

Eventually the Jefferses contacted friends who lived in the northwest part of Miami and were able to stay with them. Arriving at their friends' house at noon on Tuesday, the Jefferses dropped off their daughter and headed down south to their own neighborhood: "It was like a funeral procession, coming down, especially that first day. . . . Everybody was quiet, and you'd see these big concrete buildings down, and you thought, 'Oh, my God, did my little house survive? . . .' We had to come from [Richmond Heights] when we came off the turnpike—we came a different route. And when I saw that, that's when I broke. I'm usually a very strong person. I had to cry, because I thought, 'Oh, God, my house must be totaled.' But it wasn't." When she first saw their house, she didn't want to go in. "That was my reaction. My husband wanted to go in, but he was waiting for me. He didn't want to go in without me."[26]

Lennox Jeffers, Alicia's husband, recalled that "there was a lot of devastation, beginning from the first home on our street. So we just looked at home after home, until we got to ours, and felt somewhat relieved that it was not totally destroyed. . . . It's very hard to recreate the feelings that one has during this time. It was very emotional, very, very, emotional, because we met neighbors that stayed through the course of the hurricane, and they were able to tell us . . . whether or not our dog was alive, and things of that sort. . . . It was just an overwhelming scene."[27] The Jefferses' home was largely intact. Most of the damage had been caused by water entering the house through broken windows.

As Alicia recalled: "We had a screen around the patio, and that pulled away. Where that pulled away, that part of the roof was exposed. And that was the only structural damage. Everything else was windows down, so it was [mostly] water [damage]. I had my baby grand [piano] . . . and it was full of water . . . all of our patio furniture was in here [the living room]. And it was incredible, because the stuff must have floated around."[28]

Paul Shaffer had gone to Clearwater with his family and stayed at his brother's house throughout the hurricane. On Monday he drove back to Miami with his brother, leaving his wife and family up north:

My brother and I jumped in his convertible and drove down. We drove down with a case of beer—[we] stocked up the car on Sunday, rather, on Monday morning. We went out and bought [a] propane stove, propane gas, lantern, battery-powered lights, canned food coming out the ears—mostly Dinty Moore beef stew, no spam. My brother and I drew the line: Spam or sardines we won't eat. We'll do K-rations, but we will not do that. Oh, lots of fresh fruit—not [fresh] fruit but fruit in a can, canned fruit—and crackers coming out the ears. And loaves of bread and a lot of luncheon meats in a cooler. And we put all this stuff together, while we're arguing with Laurie about whether she's coming with us. Then we put it all in the back seat of this convertible and roared off to—oh, Gatorade, we had tons and tons of Gatorade—and we roared off to Miami, with no traffic. We didn't hit traffic until we pulled off the turnpike and 152nd Street.

Shaffer and his brother arrived at his house between 4:00 and 5:00 P.M. on Monday afternoon. They were totally amazed at the destruction they saw, despite previous experiences with natural disasters. Shaffer's brother was particularly surprised.

My older brother was not in the earthquake in Mexico City. He had been in the earthquake in Caracas with us. We lost some friends there. The destruction! He had forgotten how destructive nature can be, so he wasn't expecting it to be as bad. He thought it was going to be like the eighty-mile-per-hour winds they get in Tampa once in awhile. That's how bad it would be. . . . So he was really shocked. He just couldn't believe there were concrete electrical girders bent over and/or broken. He just stared at them. Lines down all over the place, trees destroyed, houses just blown away—152nd Street is just infamous now for the destruction.

We drove down the street; we had to weave in and out of people's yards as we tried to get toward our house. The streets were so blocked with power lines and with trees that you couldn't [drive through]—you literally had to drive up on people's lawns to drive around. Fortunately, I recognized a lot of the houses, not the landmarks that go along with it. Obviously there were no signs up. I recognized the houses enough that I got through to our own street. . . . South of 152nd Street, nobody was there, until we got to the house.[29]

Shaffer and his brother had to cut a path to the house using a machete. At the house they discovered that looters were already there.

When we got to the house, there were three people poking around our house. I tell you, I like to think at first that they weren't doing anything, but there was no explanation. We kind of pulled the car out to the side and said, "Can we help you?" One person who was almost going into the house as we came up suddenly bolted and rushed over to the car. One other person was over to the side, and another one that was over in front of him came over and said, "Well, we're just looking for a piece of plywood to put over this so we could drive by." There was plywood everywhere, right next to the car. They could have just moved it over, put it down. Since all the windows had blown out this one side, and the doors had blown open, they were getting ready to go in and see what was available. They didn't put up a fuss, they didn't do anything, they just jumped in their car and very quickly [got] out of there.

Then we started doing the inspection. We walked around first on the outside to see if there were any more people. Trying to see if there was any electricity, so we wouldn't get electrocuted. We went inside the house [to] see if there was any water. Naturally, we saw all the destruction on the east side of the house. Trees all over the place, half of them inside the swimming pool.

Most of the damage sustained by Shaffer's house probably resulted from flying debris. According to him, it

> was caused by the tile that was from the roofs behind us, because we had a three-foot pile of tile in the family room. Tile in every room practically, literally every room in the house had tile that had been blown in sometime, that had come through. . . . Most of it was from the house that had just been finished behind us, just before the storm. We checked the tiles afterwards, and we found out they hadn't even been glued—we couldn't find glue on the tile. We were getting these huge chunks of tile with no glue, and nothing to hold it down. So they were just lying . . . when they built the roof, they obviously just put the tiles right on top of each other, and the weight would hold them down. They had to rebuild it because it wasn't built to code. This is stuff that, well, you discover later.[30]

And so, as people emerged from their houses the morning following Andrew, or returned home from where they had gone to weather the storm, they had to confront the destruction caused by the hurricane. Many were simply thankful to have met the physical challenge of Andrew and to be alive. The less obvious challenges, however, were ahead. Almost everyone was going to have to survive without electricity—without air-conditioning, lights, and refrigerators—and sometimes even without water. And on top of all that, they had to begin to rebuild what was now a shattered and devastated community.

Immediate Emergency Relief

4

The evacuation of people from low-lying areas before Hurricane Andrew struck had been highly successful. During the first hundred hours after the storm, however, relief efforts proved inadequate. There were many reasons for this. A major storm had not hit South Florida since the mid-1960s, and an entire generation had grown up with no experience of hurricanes. In addition, the exceptional force of the storm and the fact that it covered an area of twenty-five to thirty miles, from downtown Miami south to Homestead, created special logistical problems.

Offices of the chief executive officer for Burger King World Headquarters after Hurricane Andrew. (Image ID: wea00531)

Many of the problems that related to mounting the initial relief effort after the storm had to do with jurisdictional disputes and administrative incompetence. Metro Dade mayor Steve Clark failed to provide leadership. The relief efforts of volunteer agencies such as the American Red Cross were not coordinated with the efforts being made by the military. There were also questions over federal versus state and local jurisdiction. All these issues contributed to the confusion and lack of effective response in the first week after Andrew.

In covering the hurricane for NBC News, I. J. Hudson said that he had seen a "combination of some of the worst coordination in the world and some of the best coordination in the world." He also saw almost total frustration change to a kind of faith, as people decided, "Yes, we are going to get out of this."[1]

Critical to the rescue operations after Hurricane Andrew were the efforts of the police and local firefighters. While the police were primarily engaged in preventing looting and helping restore order, the county's 1,200 firefighters were involved in rescue operations and in providing emergency medical services.[2]

The Police

The police played a critical role in early rescue efforts, despite the fact that there was a great deal of confusion immediately after the storm. As Jane Jones (a pseudonym), a Metro Dade police officer, explained, the situation immediately after the storm "was a mess. We didn't know what to do— who to listen to." Critical help came from officers brought in from South Carolina who had had experience dealing with Hurricane Hugo. According to Jones, their advice was of much greater value than that of many of the people who were nominally in charge. Jones soon found herself "completely ignoring" her superiors and following the suggestions of the South Carolina officers.[3]

Hurricane Andrew meant that many police officers were reassigned to the southern half of the county for special duty. Metro Dade police officer Michael Tang, for example, found himself transferred to law enforcement duties in the southern half of the county the day after the hurricane.

We were told we were going down south because that's where everything was worse. I remember it like it was yesterday. We had a field force, which consists of twelve to fifteen cars in a row, with lights and sirens going all the way down to Cutler Ridge and we—I distinctly remember this—it was dark, there were no streetlights anywhere, so it was very, very dark. With the little light we had from the car, I could begin to see houses without roofs, cars overturned. As I rode by, I was at a loss for words. I was kind of like in shock. I really didn't know what to expect when the sun came up. We got to a rendezvous point, which was directly across from the Cutler Ridge Mall. I had no idea that I was in front of the Cutler Ridge Mall until someone pointed it out, that the place with no signs that was practically leveled was the mall. . . . I didn't know what street I was on, whether I was facing north, south, east, or west, just because of the destruction there.

When the sun came up, there were some National Guardsmen out in the streets already, and I saw the Holiday Inn in Cutler Ridge with practically the whole side missing. I could see into the rooms, and I saw that across from there was a pile of rubble that used to be a Peaches Record store. . . . I'd seen pictures of places like Beirut after bombs had exploded. This area was worse than Beirut. Once I saw everything, when the sun came up, I really got a grip of, wow, we're in for it, that it was gonna be a long time rebuilding, trying to get this to where it used to be.[4]

Rescue and law enforcement efforts made Tang, and others like him, feel needed in ways that were unique in his experience as a law enforcer.

Well, for the first time, I think I felt—and it's a sad way to feel—but I think to them I was like a knight in shining armor, in several cases. Like once, we had to take food down there to some of the lower-income areas, migrant labor camps, and they were scared to come out. A lot felt they would be deported if they were found. I'll tell you one story I'll never forget. We were helping distribute food and supplies. There was one family there, they had about four babies, and when we gave them what they needed, the smile that came to their faces was incredible. Many of the people would tell me that they hadn't eaten for two days, had no water, et cetera. One child—whose, I don't know—tugged on my pant leg. All he wanted was a Coke, and we didn't have a Coke. All we had was water. But in my lunchbox I had two Cokes for myself, so I opened it and told the little boy he could have anything he wanted. I didn't want any of it. I basically didn't want to eat after this poor child begged me for a Coke. I mean, all he wanted was a Coke, and it was real hard. . . . It's kind of bringing tears to my eyes right now as I'm talking. I tell you, I went home after that day and cried. . . . We are supposed to keep our cool, but it's pretty hard, though, 'cause we're human beings.[5]

Jane Jones realized that her traditional role as a police officer was being redefined. "We suddenly became the servants, the helpers, the rescue team. We weren't out there busting people. We weren't out there answering domestic disturbances. We were helping people, distributing food, making sure they were taken care of as far as injuries. The hospitals were packed, so we dealt with a lot of injuries that might have ended up in the hospital—and basic first aid. It was a very different role for us. . . . It actually made me feel good to be out there helping." Jones sensed that people were respecting the police more than before Hurricane Andrew: "Before, we were the pigs—the ones everyone tried to hide from. We were looked upon as scum in Miami—and maybe soon will be again. But I think that what we did during the hurricane earned us a lot of respect. People who would have been out breaking the law were actually asking us for help, and we were there helping people."[6]

Hurricane Andrew redefined policing in the southern part of the county. Approximately one hundred additional officers were assigned to the Cutler Ridge Station for a minimum of a year. They were expected to understand that police work would be a little different from in the past. A more humanistic approach was required, as they were expected to respond to calls for assistance and help in matters not conceived of before the storm.

Being part of the rescue effort for officers like Tang was not only difficult and exhausting, but also complicated by the fact that so many police officers and their families were victims themselves:

We were just out there helping the people, and every now and then, you'd be really, really low, because it was just depressing and you would just see the destruction, and we were working a minimum of twelve hours. We had no days off. We had 130 officers lose their houses, from Metro Dade alone. . . . It was like no one was really there—our bodies were, but our minds were elsewhere. . . . Every now and then, when you get to a really low point, something would happen to get you back up again. One day, in the car, we saw an elderly Hispanic couple who had filled their car up with water. They came up to us and they said they wanted to donate this, but we can't find a way to donate it. So they gave it to us and we gave it away to everyone we could. . . .

It was just so tough to see people who had never thought that this would ever [happen] have to stand in line, or make a line two blocks long, just to get some bread and water. A lot of people were embarrassed to have to do this. Here were people making over thirty to forty thousand dollars a year, and had nice homes, nice cars, who thought they were set, having to get whatever we could bring to help them survive.[7]

Police officers and firefighters often found themselves providing services in their own neighborhoods, because they were also victims of the storm. As Jane Jones explained: "It was hard to be professional. It was very hard. It was hard to see your neighborhood, where you'd lived all your life, gone, and the people not knowing what to do."[8]

Hurricane Andrew created an extremely difficult but not uncommon situation for Officer Michael Laughlin and his family. After the storm he was required to work twelve-hour shifts, while his wife had to handle the dramatic changes in their daily routine and family life. Unable to find housing near Laughlin's job in the south end of the county, the family temporarily moved. "Because we have gone to twelve-hour shifts, I don't see my family. Plus, I had to move up to Broward County. So in addition to the twelve hours of work here, I have an hour travel each way, so I'm up to fourteen hours. On weekdays, on a good day, I see my kids fifteen minutes. . . . I haven't had much interaction with [my] kids since the hurricane. . . . I'm not exercising and I put on at least ten pounds."[9]

Looting

Looting became a serious problem in many neighborhoods after Hurricane Andrew. In areas isolated from police services, especially as a result of the storm, looters entered storm-damaged houses and took whatever valuables they could find. It was not uncommon to see spray-painted signs on the remains of homes: "Insured by Smith and Wesson," "Looters, All the Good Things Have Been Removed," or "You loot! We shoot!" It was common to drive through the southern half of the county and see people with pistols and hunting knives strapped to their hips. In Perrine, Loretta Landrum protected her home with a .38, while her husband carried a .357 with hollow-pointed bullets.[10]

A 7:00 P.M. curfew was established from North Kendall Drive (Southwest Eighty-eighth Street) south to the county line, effective Monday night, August 24. Dealing with looting and curfew violations was an ongoing problem during the first few weeks after the hurricane. As Michael Tang recalled:

> As the weeks went by, we began making more and more curfew arrests. If the person didn't really belong in the area, we questioned people. "What are you doing here, walking, when you live in North Dade?" Like on US 1, there were a lot of places—Circuit City was one of them—that were wide open. We began enforcing more, having more patrols throughout the neighborhoods. As far as looking for looters and people who were doing home invasions in that area, that was a big focus. We became more organized as time went on. Days we distributed food and helped care for the people, and at night we made sure everyone was squared away and where they were supposed to be.[11]

The curfew stayed in effect until November 16—nearly three months after the storm struck.[12] Widespread arrests for both curfew violations and looting were made within the first twenty-four hours after the storm on Monday; police had arrested thirty-nine looters by Tuesday morning. At the Promenade Plaza near Metrozoo, eight looters pelted two Rite-Aid Pharmacy security guards with rocks. Although an army helicopter had landed with guards at Cutler Ridge Mall on Monday afternoon, the National Guard did not arrive until shortly after midnight on Tuesday. By that time many of the stores in the mall had been looted. At Knight Bicycles in Cutler Ridge, not a single bicycle was left in the store. Before the hurricane, it had 150 bicycles in its inventory.[13]

It was sometimes extremely difficult for the police to stop the looting. As Jane Jones explained: "People were in the Winn-Dixies taking food and we were supposed to shoo them away. I don't think that I have the heart to arrest someone who is taking milk for their child. So it was like you kind of told them, 'Don't do that.' But then you'd kind of turn your back and let them do what they needed to do. Then there were the other people who were going into record stores and the Radio Shacks or whatever and taking TVs and stereos. We arrested them and were pretty hard on them."[14]

Standard security procedures were no longer in effect. Alicia Jeffers, like many others, found that her biggest worry in returning to her severely damaged house in South Dade was that her alarm system no longer worked. For her, looting "was the biggest worry. And we're not gun people. We don't believe in carrying guns. Because I have a young child, I never got a gun. . . . Instead we had the alarm system. I did borrow my friend's rifle, because I was so afraid. But it would have been dangerous for me to use it." Jeffers explained that with the looters, the maternal instinct had her asking herself: "'What if somebody got in, and we really couldn't defend ourselves?' Even though my husband was here, what could we do against another gun?"[15]

Jeffers was afraid that if she left her house unattended after Andrew, it would be looted. This feeling was experienced by many throughout Dade County. If your alarm system no longer worked because you had no electricity, and if your windows were open because it was unbearably hot and you had no air-conditioning, then you felt especially vulnerable. At night, even the streetlights were out. It was very dark throughout the county. Many people camped out in roofless houses or stayed in recreational vehicles and trailers parked in their yards, just so they could protect their remaining property. Eve Koenig explained that although it was not very convenient living in a trailer next to their house, she and her family "felt better staying on the premises because everyone in the beginning was worried about looters coming in."[16]

The National Guard

Twenty thousand National Guard troops were sent to Dade County by Governor Lawton Chiles immediately after the hurricane to help maintain law and order. They guarded shopping plazas and grocery stores. They also directed traffic on roads and highways where there were no street-lights and, many times, not even street signs.

Frank Da Silva, Jr., a captain in the National Guard, and his men were grouped in a staging area in the north end of town, where he encountered "mass confusion" as the operation got underway:

> My unit does not have that mission [riot training] because we are a specialized [intelligence] unit and we have not had that training. So the first confusion was, Here we are, what do we do? In addition to that, being a relatively new unit, we had very little of our equipment that was actually authorized. We had no vehicles, as a matter of fact. We had one two-and-one-half-ton truck and that was the extent of our equipment. We are supposed to have Humvees and all this other stuff. We had no radios yet because again we had been . . . going away to different schools and supporting different missions in various parts of the world. . . . So between not having the training, not having a street mission, and not having enough equipment, we were sitting there for a couple of hours trying to figure out exactly what we were going to do.[17]

Da Silva and his men were finally posted to work with a sister company that was assigned to the armory in Homestead. As Da Silva recalled:

> It turns out that building was just about flattened, and a couple of hours before I got there we had three or four soldiers from my company and a lieutenant in my company go down there and respond to it and try and secure the place as best as possible. . . . The building was completely down and the only thing standing was the weapons storage container. They had people try and break in there and try and steal the weapons, and they had to go down there and secure that. We had one radio at that time. We managed to get a radio, and we were in communication a little bit with the National Guard and with them

down there, and they were really screaming for reinforcements because there were only, I think, four of them at the time. Four or five
of them, and it is a large facility, or at least the fenced-in part . . . they
really couldn't hold . . . looters and people that were coming in there,
and they were really worried about the weapons.

Da Silva, in fact, never made it to Homestead but was assigned instead to
the Government Center in Cutler Ridge, where he and his men worked in
conjunction with the National Emergency Medical Team. As Da Silva explained:

> What they do is they come down to devastated areas, whether it be
> hurricane, flood, whatever, and they just set up shop with nothing.
> And the Government Center was hit real hard. All the trees were
> down, some of the second floor was caved in, and some of the rooms
> were unusable. I don't know if you've ever been down there to see
> their facilities, but what they did was they came in and they took over
> the first floor, and it's a M*A*S*H unit. Basically they set up a hospi-
> tal . . . they bring their own water, they bring their own food, they
> bring their own generators, they bring their own medical equipment
> and set up from zero. I don't know what their mission statement is,
> but I would say that within twelve to twenty-four hours they are a
> working hospital.[18]

Da Silva's group still did not have an official mission. Because patients
were in with the medical group, and the Center was the major drop-off
point for relief supplies in the area, Da Silva and his men decided to go
ahead and provide security for the building.

> All these prescription drugs and things were coming into that
> place—I don't know how many millions of dollars of equipment. . . .
> And, because our unit is basically a linguistic unit, predominantly
> Spanish, they needed the linguist assets because again this team was
> from North Carolina and very few of them—I think maybe one—
> spoke Spanish. That's basically what our mission was. They gave us
> the facility to secure—basically it was our building. We worked for

them, whatever they needed we did, but the security was ours. We set up the security as we saw fit, depending upon what their needs were.

Da Silva described the activities of the emergency medical unit.

If you've ever seen *M*A*S*H*, just take that out of military context and put it into civilian context and that was exactly what they were doing. . . . Patients were coming in one door and going out the other and left and right. In addition to that, it was a major drop-off point for supplies, equipment, and for volunteers coming down. There were an awful lot of volunteers from all across the country who were converging there, and then they would send out some from there to different areas. And that was kind of interesting at times to see all this happening and see how people would really come to the rescue. . . . I really got an opportunity to see an awful lot as opposed to being in one place doing a job.

The type of people that were coming in and the state of mind that they were in after experiencing the hurricane and being in a home that was leveled . . . some of them that came in literally hadn't eaten for two days. . . . We brought our own food down there, some meals ready to eat that everyone talked about, and we literally gave them away because people were coming in and they hadn't eaten, with four kids, and they hadn't eaten in I don't know how many hours. One of my lieutenants literally took out all of her food that we were given for the twenty-four hours, plus we get a little bit more. She just pulled it all out and started feeding some of the kids.

According to Da Silva, the medical staff at the Government Center didn't just rescue people—even a Doberman pinscher wandered into the hospital. It was very dehydrated and very tired and hungry. One of the nurses tried to feed it, but it was too exhausted to eat. A couple of hours later, the main doctor from the medical team came in and looked it over. "He put an IV into the dog, and they actually filmed it. He wasn't supposed to do it and he knew he was going to get into big trouble, especially if that hit the news media. . . . They rehydrated him with two bottles."[19] Later in the day, a couple who had come in to get tetanus shots took the dog home.

Serving in the guard was a hardship for many of Da Silva's troops, he said.

> We had soldiers in our unit who had homes and families in devastated areas. We needed to get them out because here they are, they left their homes the same morning and left their families stranded to respond to their duty, and we had to take care of that. We also had a number of full-time students, me being one of them, and they were concerned about the schools starting to reopen and not messing that up—the whole semester. What they did was . . . an order-of-priority list of people. First, who had damaged homes and families, and then full-time students, and then third on that list . . . are people with job problems . . . for instance, the guys in devastated areas; . . . we went to them and said, "Okay, you're on the list. You can go home and take care of your family." They said, "Well, I have no job now, so leave me on active duty and I'll get paid."[20]

Da Silva and his troops were eventually assigned to field duties in which they had the opportunity to use their cross-cultural and linguistic skills. His unit was not completely deactivated until November.

By September 8, 6,257 National Guardsmen were in South Florida.[21] Some of them camped out at Eve Koenig's school, Palmer-Trinity on Southwest 176th Street. She recalls that they used the campus as their headquarters and even participated in the opening-day ceremonies "in the raising of the flag. You could have heard a pin drop. It was outside because we no longer have our gymnasium where we usually hold our assemblies, and it was unbelievably quiet." Alicia Jeffers said she and her husband, Lennox, also welcomed the National Guard's presence: "The [National Guard] were [coming] through here, though, and we made friends with the Guards, so they would protect us."[22]

Kate Hale Calls in the Cavalry

President George H. W. Bush personally responded to the crisis in South Florida by coming to view the damage twelve hours after Hurricane Andrew struck. At 6 P.M. on August 24, *Air Force One* landed at Opa Locka

Airport in the northern end of the county. Accompanied by Governor Lawton Chiles, Senator Connie Mack, and Congresswoman Ileana Ros-Lehtinen, the president proceeded south by motorcade, stopping on Miller Drive in South Dade to examine an uprooted tree and then going on to Cutler Ridge Mall. In Cutler Ridge, the president made a speech in front of a Peaches Record Store that had been looted after the storm. At one point, the stunned president mumbled, "Horrible."[23] After spending only a couple of hours in South Florida, Bush was rushed back to the airport and his return flight to Washington, D.C.[24] Broward, Dade, and Monroe Counties had been declared disaster areas.

The federal government was very slow to provide relief. The crisis caused by Andrew came to a head on Thursday, August 27, when Kate Hale, the Dade County emergency director, demanded, with tears welling in her eyes, "Where in the hell is the cavalry?" By this time, more than 250,000 storm victims were struggling to survive without food, water, or shelter. Live, on radio and national television, Hale's anger erupted over the slowness of the government to provide aid:

> I want this live. Enough is enough. Quit playing like a bunch of kids.
> ... Where in the hell is the cavalry? For God's sakes, where are they?
> We're going to have more casualties, because we're going to have more people dehydrated. People without water. People without food. Babies without formula. We need food, we need water, we need people down here. We're all about ready to drop, and the reinforcements are not going in fast enough. We need better National Guard down here. They do not take orders from me. . . . I'm not the disaster czar down here. President Bush was down here. I'd like him to follow up on the commitments he made."[25]

Later that day President Bush finally deployed 30,000 troops to the South Dade area. He returned to South Florida on September 1 as extensive criticism concerning the federal government's slow response to the crisis continued to mount.[26]

Lieutenant General Samuel Ebbesen, once chief of staff for General Norman Schwarzkopf, was placed in charge of the army's relief effort in South Florida. As leader of 14,400 troops, Ebbesen said his primary task was to provide hurricane victims with food and water and then to help clear the debris left by the storm.[27] Like everyone else, the military was stunned by what they saw. According to Master Sergeant Lester Richardson, who had spent six months in the Middle East during Desert Storm, "This is worse than anything we saw in Saudi. These people need a miracle."[28]

Military relief efforts, once they began, were extensive. Marines from Camp LeJeune, North Carolina, came to set up tent cities for those who had been left homeless by the storm.[29] A week after the hurricane, on Monday, August 31, the USS *Sylvania* arrived off the coast of South Florida. Sent from Norfolk, Virginia, the *Sylvania,* which normally provides cargo support for aircraft carriers, held the equivalent of 137 boxcars of provisions—enough food to take care of 30,000 soldiers for a month. By Thursday, the ship and its crew were able to airlift breakfast, via helicopter, to 2,400 people.[30] By September 8, 22,271 U.S. troops were in the area, with additional troops on the way.[31] It was to become the largest U.S. military rescue mission in history.[32] By the end of their tour of duty, the military had given away ten thousand radios with batteries and delivered generators, mobile hospitals, and other crucial supplies. They had set up tents for refugees at Harris Field and in a park in Homestead, removed fallen trees in Cutler Ridge, and patrolled mobile-home parks in Homestead. David Jones, whose Florida City home was destroyed by Andrew, noted: "You don't ever get to see the military help you directly. You just hear about them fighting in places. This is what they ought to do."[33]

But some Florida National Guard members resented the federal troops. Frank Da Silva, for example, recalled that when the Eighty-second Airborne arrived, they had an attitude. "Granted they're warriors and they're taught to have an attitude and in combat you have to have an attitude or else you're gonna die, but when they come down, sometimes they exhibit themselves. They really treat the National Guard, first of all, like they're nothing. . . . The only reason that I got any of the little respect that I did is because I had Airborne wings on my chest, and I'm a paratrooper. . . . Other than that they treated all of my people like dirt."[34]

The Eighty-second Airborne Division set up their command post at the Government Center in Cutler Ridge. Although most of the building was destroyed, Da Silva said, "there were a couple of courtrooms there that were useable, and they decided to make their offices in those courtrooms. . . . I don't think the medical team liked it too much. . . . They [Eighty-second Airborne] came in, decided that this was [their] headquarters and we're going to take whatever we need. We had confrontations with them due to that; . . . the only way you could get up was go through the lobby to the second floor where they wanted to take over. And we had injured people and medical people and supplies and everything going in and out all over the place."[35]

Emergency Medical Facilities

Field hospitals were quickly set up in South Dade after Hurricane Andrew. In Homestead, local doctors and paramedics, together with medical teams from Indiana and South Carolina, converted a senior citizens' center into an emergency field hospital. At the South Dade Government Center in Cutler Ridge, office space was converted into an emergency medical center.[36]

Palmetto General Hospital set up a field clinic in a private house near Harris Field. Armando Santelices, a specialist in general surgery, found himself doing everything at this center, "from a blood pressure check on somebody who feels anxiety to a baby that's two months old with meningitis, a lot of lacerations, a lot of infections, a lot of diabetics with infection, the gamut. I had a pregnant woman who almost delivered. . . . Someone who was working on a roof fell off the roof. . . . You name it, we've done it."[37] After working fourteen-hour days, Santelices had to drive north to Broward County to get home for the night.

Bill Blackburn, a nurse who belonged to the Eighteenth Airborne Corps, Fort Bragg, North Carolina, was billeted at Homestead Senior High School but worked at the medical facility at Harris Field. Called up on the Thursday after the hurricane, he was given less than two hours to pack his gear, say goodbye to his family, and head south on an air transport.

Once he arrived, Blackburn began treating people for rashes, cuts, diarrhea, cramps, and related minor illnesses. In particular, he needed to help people resume regular dosage of their various medications, which they either had lost as a result of the storm or needed to be refilled. Diabetics, for example, were frequently in need of special help, Blackburn said. "Diabetics are coming in here unable to eat proper diets. They have sky-high blood sugars. We're not able to treat them; we don't have insulin. . . . We send them up the road."[38] Blackburn was working seventeen to eighteen hours a day. The destruction he saw, he said, was unlike anything he had ever seen or even thought possible.

Federal Emergency Management Assistance

The Federal Emergency Management Assistance Agency (FEMA) was severely criticized after Hurricane Andrew for its failure to deal effectively with the crisis. Established in 1979 by President Jimmy Carter as an independent agency, FEMA's job is to supervise civil defense, disaster relief, fire prevention, earthquake hazard reduction, emergency broadcasting services, flood insurance, homeless shelters, and dam safety. At the time the hurricane hit, FEMA had the largest ratio of political appointees to federal government employees of any federal agency. Throughout much of its brief history, the agency had been criticized not only for incompetence, but also for graft and corruption.[39]

During the first three or four days following the hurricane, FEMA's response proved totally inadequate. Conflicts arose over jurisdiction and funding as people in hurricane-devastated neighborhoods waited for relief efforts to arrive. According to Scott Higham, who analyzed the agency's efforts after the storm: "The agency was slow to respond. It ran confusing relief programs. It failed to foresee the ferocity of the storm and plan ahead. It didn't conduct early damage assessments, hobbling the flow of food, water and medical supplies to the hardest hit areas."[40]

James White, working out of the federally funded Family Adolescent and Development Center, was assigned by FEMA to do general counseling with hurricane victims in the first few weeks after the storm. In White's opinion: "FEMA was not prepared for Hurricane Andrew. They weren't prepared to work with special populations such as the migrant workers, the poor, and the elderly. I believe there needs to be a contingency plan. I think that they need to start now to put together a network of people that could provide psychological services, who would be willing to go down into the areas affected by hurricanes like Andrew; . . . actually all this networking [should be] set up before the catastrophe occurs."[41]

Roberta Smith recalls what happened when she asked FEMA for assistance:

> Well, I went to get help. You know they were telling you about FEMA and stuff. So I went, and they told me to find a place to stay and they'll pay the first month's rent to help me out. I did what those people told me to do. I looked for a place, found one, got the form they told me to get, filled it out, and took it back to the lady. Lord, those lines you had to wait in. I waited again in that long line, and you know what that lady told me, that FEMA couldn't help me. I looked [her] straight in the eye and told her: "I came to you for help telling the truth and you have people lying to you and you give them all the help they need. They weren't the ones that needed help." But I had to stand on faith that the Lord would never forsake me or leave me, and he didn't. I was provided for, and I'm still here without FEMA's help.[42]

Volunteers in South Dade

Hurricane Andrew generated a massive volunteer effort on the part of people both in Florida and from elsewhere in the country. As Art Carlson commented, there were a "staggering number of volunteers that flowed down into the area immediately afterwards, not just sightseers, but volunteers that went down there with food, clothing, anything they could to get down there. And you knew there were going to be rip-off artists down there, and everyone was warning everyone else about that, but just the number of volunteers that were down there, . . . that came from out of state, the convoys of people and volunteers—it was staggering. I've never seen anything like that in my life."[43]

Many local people who had suffered relatively little damage to their own homes went down to South Dade to help in the recovery efforts. For days immediately after the storm, they distributed food and water, directed traffic at intersections without traffic lights, and even helped repair roofs. Unfortunately, much of the volunteer relief effort was very primitive. The needed organization often just wasn't there. Whoever could come to help, came. It wasn't run like a business, so many of the relief supplies were simply distributed on a first-come, first-served basis.

More than three hundred volunteer nurses arrived in South Florida in the first few days after Andrew to provide help in the relief effort. Trish Tate, a pediatric nurse who had arrived from Jacksonville on the Thursday after the storm, roamed the streets in Goulds. There she provided children with basic medical care, as well as vaccinations against diseases such as diphtheria, polio, meningitis, measles, mumps, and rubella.[44] Ross McGill recalled how the Boy Scouts helped to distribute food in the disaster area: "We had volunteers unloading water and food, and getting food distributed. We were involved in numerous clearing projects, helping to distribute equipment that we owned."[45]

Ronald V. Ponton went down to Homestead as part of his ministry as a Jehovah's Witness. Along with his wife and two children, he got up every morning at 4:00 A.M. to head down south to the Homestead and Perrine area, where the organization had set up mobile kitchens. They worked together as a family and were able to accomplish a lot by helping "over three thousand families who had homes that were damaged to get their homes straightened out. What we did was work in a centralized mobile kitchen that provided food for the workers. These were men that came from as far as New Jersey, Louisiana, and North Carolina to help in the relief work. We cooked breakfast, lunch, and dinner for them. We did this for as many as five hundred to seven hundred at a time."[46]

The Jehovah's Witnesses were one of the first groups to begin relief efforts. Even before the storm hit, they had tractor trailers on their way down to South Florida, bringing lumber, tar paper, and other supplies. Personally viewing the impact that the storm had on people particularly affected Ponton. "We had only seen it on TV and we thought what had taken place was awful. But to actually see it, and see it as people talked, you could sense the distress in them and in some of the depressed ones and how they were affected by it."[47]

Three thousand Jehovah's Witnesses from across the country came to help in the relief effort. From their headquarters at Kingdom Hall on 216th Street in Homestead, they spread out to help take down 174 trees, clean 322 homes, repair 579 different structures, and rebuild 49 homes.[48]

For Ponton: "It was really spiritually and emotionally faith strengthening. As we were helping people, they couldn't believe that others could come together and assist one another. As we were working in one house of Jehovah's Witnesses, we would assist neighbors who weren't of the same religion in a house nearby. This really brought the people together. Helping in the kitchen and preparing food was a relief, because these people came to work and they wouldn't have to worry about food and a place of rest because all of that was provided for them."[49]

Other religious groups also volunteered to help people in the South Dade area. The Southern Baptists served 80,000 meals a day at the height of the relief effort. The Greater Miami Jewish Federation transported 250,000 pounds of food into the area. The United Methodist Committee on Relief had teams come in from around the country to help distribute food and rebuild churches.

It was the network of black churches and ministries operating in Richmond Heights that provided Roberta Smith with the help that she needed, she said. "The black people in Richmond Heights were real good to one another during this time. You know the white man didn't help us. It was the people down there that got out and walked from door to door letting us know where to get food and stuff. The churches down there was real good about helping folk out. They fed us, provided shelter if you needed it, and gave you clothes if you didn't have any."[50]

To a large degree, informal relief efforts were more effective during the first stages of the crisis than the efforts of more traditional relief agencies such as the American Red Cross. Lawrence Moose described how the inability to "get relief efforts rolling" made people like him feel helpless at first. "It was a very helpless feeling on Monday when the storm had passed. You were . . . ready to go in there and really work hard to get food to the shelters and feed these people and make sure that everyone was okay . . . [and] the suppliers you had contracted with just couldn't help you. They couldn't get trucks out. They couldn't get into facilities that they owned." Unforeseen problems occurred. The fact that the electricity was off throughout much of the county meant that some suppliers could not get into their warehouses where relief supplies were stored. "In one case, they had an electronic lock system that actually locked them out of their own facility. . . . And of course, truckers were not reporting to work because they had their own problems; . . . it was an unfortunate learning experience where we learned what their real capabilities were versus what we thought they were going to be. . . . That first day was really, really a terrible feeling of helplessness."[51]

Probably no one was more upset over the logistical snafus than the Red Cross. Given limited resources, the magnitude of the crisis, and lack of recent experience with hurricanes in the area, it was almost impossible for the Red Cross to function effectively. As Moose saw it:

> We haven't had a storm in a long time. A lot of people out in the community were apathetic toward hurricanes, believing they didn't happen and when they did, they weren't going to be nearly as destructive as this one. Maybe our vendors suffered from the same feeling as the majority of the public. I'm not saying that we knew how big it was going to be or how bad or that our planning, had it been executed right, would have been any better. But we certainly know now for the future. It's a tough lesson. . . . That was a tough period personally. I remember feeling so frustrated. It's a terrible feeling to want to help and feeling like you have the resources but you can't do anything."[52]

Sometimes the "aid" itself was the problem. Pat Ashley, a Presbyterian pastor, recalls that "people came down and unloaded diapers in the big room. We don't need diapers here, so I either had to let them sit there not being used or use my time to figure out how to get them someplace else. They were so proud of themselves for getting down here with this stuff. It was like . . . it didn't help me!"[53]

Damien Kong firmly believed that if it weren't for the food sent from up north, many of the zoo employees would not have made it through the weeks after Andrew. They received donations of everything from monkey biscuits to clothes: "We had literally our whole hay barn full of clothes . . . my wife right now is wearing some of the clothes that we got as donations from the hurricane. Pretty good clothes. Some were not so good, too. But we tried our best to sort what was good out. We had a lot of fun doing that, too. You'd be surprised what people wore. [Laughter] Some of the things were pretty raunchy." At the same time, Kong couldn't believe what some people had donated—even a used toothbrush. "I mean we're desperate, but we're not that desperate."[54]

Corporate Aid

Some of the best aid—targeted specifically to what people really needed and delivered quickly—came from local corporations. Carolyn Donaldson said that Cordis Corporation provided aid to its employees in a number of ways.

> We immediately set up an emergency bank service to provide check cashing and cash advances to our employees. We sent out search parties looking for employees that we had not heard from or contacted. All of our employees were paid for all time off during that period of time. We provided temporary housing by making available our corporate apartments as well as a number of employees providing shelter in their own homes. We set up an emergency store so that employees could come and shop, because a lot of stores were not operating due to the storm.[55]

Cordis also conducted a food drive for South Dade.

One of the products Tony Sardinas's company, Bayshore Equipment Distributing, sold was ice machines. The company's factory, which is located in Illinois, donated several 1,400–pound machines with bins and a large generator. Bayshore then distributed the machines to several facilities, including the Salvation Army, which had large enough generators to run them. Once Bayshore got its power back, it was able to run its own machines and make bundles of ice for distribution in South Dade, mostly at the tent cities, where the ice went directly to the military for distribution. The employees had also taken up a collection to buy formula, Pampers, wipes, and so on, and these supplies were dropped off with the ice.[56]

The Gainesville office of Liberty Mutual Insurance Company sent close to two hundred boxes of food and clothing supplies to its Miami office. The local office of the company was given an expense account to buy food items, water, and generators. When policyholders came into the office, they were given whatever they wanted or needed. Lehman Brothers in Miami raised funds for relief for their own employees and for the needs of those in South Dade. The firm also participated in the Adopt-a-Family program that was developed at its New York headquarters. Throughout the country, Lehman employees could sign up to adopt a family in South Florida. A designated amount would automatically be deducted from the employee's paycheck to help support the local family.

While the main thrust of Florida Power and Light's efforts after Andrew was simply to get the power back on throughout Dade County, its Human Resources Department focused on employees' needs, mental as well as physical. They sent out information on trauma symptoms. Teams of employees were organized to volunteer on Saturdays to help other employees who had lost their homes.[57]

On Wednesday, August 26, two days after Andrew, only two to three hundred of the more than one thousand employees of American Bankers Insurance Group, Inc., on Quail Roost Drive in South Dade managed to make it to work. Tuesday would have been their normal payday. They were told: "Don't worry, those of you that have direct deposit, your paychecks are deposited. Those of you whose checks are mailed, we have them over here on the patio." They were standing in a building with most of its windows blown out and almost everything inside trashed by the wind. And yet they were also told, "You won't be doing your normal job, but you all have jobs." Things got much worse at American Bankers once the rains came at the end of the week. The rain and the falling ceiling tiles did extensive damage to much of their equipment, and that is when everything turned to "ceiling tile mud," according to Melinda Smith, a video specialist at the company. Despite suffering such a disaster, the company stayed in business, paid claims, and even managed to sign on new accounts. They discovered, said Smith, that "the company is not the building, it's the people. And they're some pretty terrific people, because look at what we've accomplished."[58]

Opening Up the Tent Cities

By the Saturday after Hurricane Andrew, relief crews were scrambling to build tent cities in Homestead for approximately 5,000 people.[59] The first tent city to be opened was at Harris Field on Campbell Drive in Homestead. The encampment, which included a civilian eating area, toilets, mobile kitchens, a medical aid station, and free long-distance telephone services, could accommodate 1,500 people.[60]

Many people were reluctant to move from their neighborhoods into the tent cities. Wanting to protect what little they had left in their damaged homes from looters and not trusting the military were just a few of the reasons they gave for hesitating to leave their hurricane-ravaged neighborhoods. A particular problem was that many illegally documented workers were afraid to seek help because they feared they would be deported.

Many of the workers in the tent cities were volunteers. Amy Moss, for example, a sixteen year old from Newport, Kentucky, came down to South Dade immediately after Andrew with a friend who was a roofer. After working for a while at the Homestead City Hall, she was assigned to the kitchen at Harris Field. As she explained, her reason for coming down was simply "to help."[61]

A month after the storm, eight hundred people remained in tent cities in the southern part of the county.[62] They were primarily the poorest and least able to cope with the financial and personal disasters imposed by the hurricane.[63]

Despite relief efforts on the part of volunteer groups, corporations, local, state, and federal agencies, the National Guard, and the military, almost everyone in Dade County realized that they would have to fend for themselves. The rebuilding of lives, houses, and businesses, while aided by groups from the outside, was ultimately something everyone soon discovered they had to handle on their own.

The First Weeks

5

For most people, the first days and weeks after Hurricane Andrew were best described by a T-shirt spotted in South Dade with the message: "I survived Hurricane Andrew, but the rebuilding is killing me!" Rebuilding after such massive destruction would have been a difficult task under normal conditions. Rebuilding while under curfew, without electricity, and without proper transportation was even more of a challenge for a physically and psychologically stressed population.

For some people, the luckier ones whose houses had survived and who had come through the storm intact, the first week after the hurricane was

Two vehicles overturned by the force of the wind in a garage. (Image ID: wea00532)

filled with back-breaking labor—putting their houses back in order and cleaning up their yards and neighborhoods. Elizabeth Garcia Granados's experience was fairly typical. "The first week was a lot of hard physical labor because of the cleanup of the debris and the tree cutting and that sort of thing. But also, as you recall, we were in the hot season. . . . It was hot and muggy. We had no air-conditioning, no telephone, no electricity, and to get a hot meal was kind of an ordeal. There wasn't enough ice in town. . . . We had to eat out of cans for almost a month. To get a hot cup of coffee was a real luxury in the morning."[1]

Bonnie Sheil, a teacher at Bowman Foster Ashe Elementary School, remembers: "I had no electricity, no water. The worst camp-out I've ever been on! It was terrible!" Sheil said that trying to get things done was unusually hard, that it seemed as though everything was in "slow motion."[2]

Logistics were a nightmare in the first weeks after the storm. People in the southern end of the county often had to travel twenty to thirty miles on roads that had been severely damaged and covered with debris in order to get tools and building supplies. Most traffic lights still were not working. Everyone was stressed out. Problems that would have seemed minor under normal circumstances became major issues. Karen Baldwin's husband, Scott, lost his only pair of eyeglasses when they were blown off his face during the storm. Unable to replace them, he found himself having to drive his car while barely able to see the road.

Karen went through several different stages during the first week after the storm.

> After the uniqueness of the experience wears off, we went through a real energy surge—"We've got to get this cleaned up." Everybody, the whole neighborhood, was the same way. "Oh, this neighbor lost shingles, so we've got to paper over their roof. Well, I've got a friend that has paper, I'll see if I can get in contact with them. We'll get the paper, we'll paper his roof. Does the guy across the street need paper? Fine, we've got extra paper." Everybody is helping everybody else. There is this frantic activity all in the house, all up and down the street, to make immediate repairs, to keep things going. And you've got energy to do it, and you're kind of empowered to get this stuff done. We had a neighborhood barbecue. . . . Everybody put their food

together . . . threw everything on the barbecue. . . . We happened to have a Coleman camper stove . . . so we were making coffee. People were walking around dying for a cup of coffee a day or so after the storm.[3]

In the authors' neighborhood, a retired university professor in her early nineties was able to provide that early morning coffee because she had the only propane gas stove on the block.

Chain saws and portable electrical generators became highly sought-after commodities. Lennox Jeffers recalled that he was given a number for purchasing a generator and had to return on successive days to Home Depot until one was available: "You had to stand in line, and we were number fourteen. At 7 A.M. in the morning, we were number fourteen, waiting for generators, 'cause the new batch [had] come in. I don't want to see another Home Depot for awhile. . . . Every morning, that was our routine. We'd go to the Miami Lakes Home Depot, you know, stand in line for a generator or something else we needed—you know, we were trying to prepare for when Mom and Dad and everybody came down—what we would need, a chain saw, or this, or that. And they brought down a lot of stuff, too, thank God. And we would make the long trek down—it was like a funeral procession, coming down."[4]

During the first week after the storm, Mike Brescher recalled:

We didn't have any electricity so the touch-tone phones don't work without electricity. So my mother-in-law has one of the old dial phones, she never was much for technology, so we hooked that up. But we could only call long distance. So we would call my brother-in-law and sister, and they would call the airports and make ticket reservations for the women, and then we would get them to the airport. They would all go up north to various places. My mom went up to Chicago, and my mother-in-law went up to Jersey. And the neighbors went to Detroit . . . just tried to get them all in different places away from here. . . . Then the sons came down. My brother-in-law came down, his sons came down.

The main thing was that we were going through freezers and houses to gather up what we could. We were barbecuing everything.

We lived off of the grill. We would search houses for propane tanks for the grills. All the food and heat came from the grills. The gas was mostly the only thing left of the houses, so we would use it since no one else was. We were just trying to get things squared away and survive day by day.

Mike noticed that the weird part of that first week was that if you had water for that day, you were grateful. "You never thought about the day after this one, just one by one."[5]

Melinda Smith, who lived in Coconut Grove and worked for American Banker's Insurance Company in Perrine, found the week after the storm "one of the most difficult weeks I have ever gone through. That week . . . well, the first couple of days were just spent cleaning up around here, just to be able to get out of the neighborhood. Then that Wednesday I think was the hardest day, because that Wednesday we were supposed to go back to work. . . . I went back to work, and that was when I drove into disaster land." Melinda was encouraged by her supervisor to help a fellow worker and close friend, Debbie (who lived in the devastated Country Walk complex), get back to work as quickly as possible. So Wednesday afternoon Melinda got in her car and "went to her house and saw . . . how . . . it was like a bomb had gone off in Country Walk. You know, driving . . . a four-wheel vehicle down the sidewalk and across the median and down part of the street for awhile, and then up the sidewalk and back down again. . . . I've been to Debbie's house numerous times, but I had no inkling how to find her house, because like most drivers, I drive by landmarks. I know at this stop sign or whatever, I make a left. And then I know I make the first left past this little shopping center on the right or whatever. And none of these landmarks were there."[6]

For many people who lived in the southern part of the county, so much of what they took for granted was gone: no toilets, no water, no air-conditioning, no food, no sanitation, and so on. If you didn't have electricity, you didn't have an alarm system, and you could forget about trying to secure your house when you were trying to get people to come in and work on it. Back-up security arrangements for just such an emergency fell through when you couldn't even locate back-up guards for apartment and condominium complexes.

Damien Kong spent most of the first week after Andrew cleaning up at Metrozoo.

The classrooms that I worked in and our office building were just totally destroyed. The roofs went off, and there was a lot of water damage. So we spent most of the time trying to salvage what we could out of the classrooms and the offices, trying to salvage what we could with the animals that we had in the classroom and in what we call an ark. The ark is our building in which we maintain all the animals for the education department and for the petting zoo, which is pretty extensive. We've got quite a few animals. None of the roofs were actually *lost* lost. It was just a lot of damage and a lot of water coming in. So we spent a lot of time making sure the animals were secured. Some of us took some of the animals home just to make sure that they were taken care of.[7]

Many people found the first week following the storm both emotional and stressful. Patricia Whitely, the associate director for Residential Life and Staff Development at the University of Miami recalls neither fear nor desperation after the hurricane, but instead a "tremendous sadness." Surprising emotions came to the surface for her: "I remember on Friday of that week, I was on the phone with my parents . . . in New York and I started sobbing, really crying . . . I was crying about the zoo. The fact of the matter is that I've never even been to the zoo. It's not like I'm in with the zebras or anything, but I felt really sad about the area, about what it means to us, for the university. I've lived here eleven years. Tremendous stress, 'I can't believe this is happening to me.' Those were some of the feelings I had."[8]

Some of the challenges faced by people after the hurricane were unique. Edward T. Foote II, president of the University of Miami, was confronted by the problem of how to get the university back into operation for the school year. After the storm he found himself trying to "stay level-headed, think carefully, to keep emotion out of it, to try to understand what the priorities are. . . . The first few days I spent thinking how we could resume functioning again; . . . we had a real crisis on our hands. . . . How could we make emergency decisions but then get school open again? Should we close down? Should we send them home? . . . What would be necessary to clean up? How were [we] to clean up eight hundred exploded windows before the heavy rains came?" Finding out whether all the members of the university community were safe became a major task in the first week after the storm. Foote asked Roy Nirscel, vice-president for University Advancement, to organize a phone bank,

> which they did. We got alumni and students to do two things. First, we tried to phone every single member of the university family to find out how they were doing, and secondly, to get volunteers, not just for the university, but to coordinate efforts for the greater Miami area. So we had the food-distribution center over here at the cafeteria. In a short period of time we had an inventory of all of our people, and those who we couldn't telephone, we found using alternative ways . . . I finally sent the police out in search parties to find the last handful.[9]

Complexes like Country Walk, where Melinda Smith had gone to help her friend Debbie, were completely torn apart by the storm. Cheap construction had made the houses particularly vulnerable to the enormous forces unleashed by Andrew. After the storm, more than 90 percent of Country Walk was uninhabitable. It was in such areas that one of the most interesting social aspects of the recovery first appeared—signs spray-painted on the sides and roofs of houses. Many signs included an insurance company's name and the owner's policy number. Often the signs were accompanied by a message to a friend or relative. "HART WE ARE ALIVE!" was the message sprayed on the garage door of one house, while next to the front door, in large letters, was the policy number for the owner's insurance.

Besides insurance information, humorous and angry comments were often expressed. A painted palm tree was decorated with a sign that read "LIFE BEGINS AFTER ANDREW." Next to it was "ARVIDA BUILT SUCKS!" which was a reference to the developer's motto, "Arvida Built." "Gone with the Wind," was one of the literary references that appeared on the signs.

Another sign advertised that the house it was painted on was for sale: "Re-Designed—Decorated—Landscaped By Hurricane Andrew Incorporated." One sign declared that the house it was painted on was being "Protected By Smith & Wesson." A skull and crossbones was included to suggest that looters would be dealt with harshly. A sign on Southwest 147th Street showed a comic figure with its tongue sticking out and an accompanying message: "you loot we shoot."

Many messages, such as "We Beat Andrew!!" reflected the determination and grit of the survivors of the hurricane. Others reflected spiritual and religious beliefs, such as "Jesus Saves!" Some of the signs quoted Scripture. On one wall a sign declared: "And his Angels encamped around those who loved the Lord." On a house on 141st Place, a sign was printed over the front door in large block letters: "God Stalks You Into Deep Waters Not To Drown You But To Teach You How To Swim."

Getting to Know the Neighbors

After Hurricane Andrew, almost everyone throughout the county reached out to those closest at hand—their neighbors. People who had lived next door to each other for years, or just a couple of houses away from one another, often met and talked for the first time, establishing a new sense of community. Soloman Graham believes that Andrew brought people together in his South Miami neighborhood.

> Maybe fear brings people closer, makes them feel different about others . . . but it seemed like the whole neighborhood was a little more [together]. Like you see everybody, they pass and say, "Hello, how you doing? What happened to you?" This and that. People is speakin' and wavin' to those who they'd never speak and wave to before. And really everybody was just, like, really sticking together, trying to do what they can for the next person. Because there was no water and electricity, and if you'd never been in that situation before, it is something to be in. And it was amazing."[10]

James McCoy, a veterinarian, noticed the same phenomenon.

> When the power was out, people came out of their houses and they talked to each other like it probably was when my parents were growing up. There was no air-conditioning running, so people came out because it was cooler outside. . . . There was no television to distract

them . . . people communicated, people went out of their way to help each other. When you got a group of people together, someone would go get ice, and they would bring ice back for other people. Or somebody would have a refrigerator working and they would help store food, or if you had a barbecue, and you had your grill going, people would come over and cook their food on your grill and then take it home and eat for the next couple of days. . . .

Everybody got along real well, you got a chance to get to know people a little bit more. If you eliminate the air-conditioning and you eliminate the television, people find that they need the entertainment and the communication and friendship of other people and they'll come out and talk, and that is neat.[11]

In some neighborhoods, neighbors went from house to house, helping each other clean up the mess. They rented trucks and moved furniture and whatever could be saved to temporary housing. James White felt that the storm had a mysterious way of uniting people: "They have helped one another, and they continue to help one another."[12]

As someone who so often had to report about the darker side of the community, Art Carlson found the new sense of community heartening. "The most positive [thing] that I could see was how incredible the community came together. I mean, all we see is the murder, the destruction, the rip-offs, and things like that, and it was so incredible, the first couple of days especially. People were actually pleasant to you on the road, they were courteous, they waited for you if there was a light . . . no light . . . or anything like that."[13]

That first week was torture for Alexis Martinez. "I mean, being . . . a city boy and used to the good life, I mean the air-conditioning everyday. I'm used to not having to go through trouble cooking, cleaning, and doing other things. The first week was definitely a challenge, but it was good, because it provided for a [chance] to stick together with the family and friends. It made us consider what life is really all about. Life is not all about just having material things. It is more of a spiritual [thing], and just believing in good things and helping one another out."[14]

Small Pleasures and Real Needs

As long as the electricity was out, ice was very hard to come by—for some, it became the stuff that dreams are made of. Melinda Smith recalled that after standing in line for most of Tuesday, the day after the storm, waiting to get ice, she tried again on Thursday. She was in line by "seven o'clock or seven thirty in the morning, and they said there would be no ice available until noon. I said, 'Screw it.' I'm not going to stand in that sort of line. So . . . I decided I would go to Broward to get ice, and I drove around Broward for five hours . . . and I couldn't find ice." Smith regrets not having played on people's guilt in Broward in order to get ice. "Had I known that the survivor guilt was as strong as it was in Broward, I'd have hit the restaurants or the hotels and played the victim role."[15]

When a friend arrived at Karen Baldwin's house with a bag of ice a few days after the storm, she thought it was like a gift "from heaven." "This was the first cold, really cold, item we had seen since Sunday night. . . . It was incredible how much a simple bag of ice could mean to somebody. Another friend dropped by with a cooler that had cold soft drinks in it . . . just to stand and drink a cold soda—incredible."[16]

Throughout the southern part of the county, many people were on well water rather than city water. Without electricity, their well pumps would not work. Karen Baldwin desperately wanted her water supply restored because, without water,

> you could not clean up, because we're all on wells here, and we had no electricity to work the pumps, we couldn't get the water. And you hesitated to use water that you had stored up for drinking purposes, or bathing purposes, or even flushing purposes . . . because you weren't sure when you were going to have water available. . . . You really couldn't clean up any of the mess that was in the house, whether it was leaves stuck to the ceilings and walls, or sand—literally sand—and mud that been blown in that was all over the place, and debris. So the one thing that became more important than anything else was the water supply.

A friend who used to live in South Florida managed to bring Karen and her family a generator on the Friday after the storm. Karen remembers that

> once the generator kicked in, it was like heaven, because we had the water to wash with. You could wash off walls or floors. You could clean yourself up a little bit. . . . There's a high priority on deodorant down here. . . . Even the idea of drinking water . . . we did drink the well water . . . taking a chance here in drinking the water, but the water coming from the well was so cold and tasted so good. It was a matter of, "We'll take the risk." Once that water kicked in, it was like you got a shot in the arm. All of a sudden, the energy build-up was back.[17]

"Is Everything Back to Normal?"

As everyone was desperately trying to cope and trying to decide what needed to be done first, they also had to contend with the outside world. There were relatives to call, if they were lucky enough to still have phone service. Calls to and from family meant a lot—a chance to talk about the details of living through Andrew and a chance to describe what it was like to just get through the day. Patricia Whitely was struck "by the number of calls I received from colleagues at other universities who called or faxed to check on us. They offered everything."[18] Many people found themselves calling local friends they had not spoken to for months, even years, just to find out how they were doing. Hurricane Andrew did not just bring neighborhoods together, it renewed friendships.

But toward the end of that first week, as more relatives could get through and business associates began calling from around the country, many South Floridians began hearing, over and over again, the question that was guaranteed to infuriate them: "Is everything back to normal now?"

Perhaps even worse than being asked if things were back to normal was not being asked. All of us have stories about the relatives who did not call, who just assumed that we were okay since they knew we did not live in Homestead. Even if you were okay, you wanted to be asked. After feeling so vulnerable, it was important to know that your friends and relatives cared enough to bother to find out how you were doing. And it was important that they listen, even if they were tired of hearing your tales of woe. We will never forget a long-distance call we received at the end of that first week when a relative from up north who didn't realize that he could be heard from the background exclaimed, "Are those people still whining?"

Stress was the norm for almost everyone throughout the county. They were surrounded by destruction, had little or no services available, and were physically exhausted. Many people had to go back to work, where things also needed to be fixed up and put back in order. Lauren Markoff, a Montessori teacher, was living in the south end of the county in an apartment that had extensive water damage. For Lauren, things were still not "back to normal" several months after Andrew.

> Many things need to be fixed. The complex is horrible. There is just debris and destruction everywhere I look. The problems in the complex are not getting any attention from the management. I feel stuck here. There is nowhere else to go. The traffic is horrendous where I live. My job was relocated to another school. Then we went back into a school that wasn't ready. Everyone that I work with and all the children that I have are traumatized and devastated. . . . I was hit by a government van. Somebody was tired, wasn't looking where he was going, and smashed into my car. I haven't been reimbursed. The car isn't fixed. Everything has changed. My mechanic isn't there anymore. I am out of touch with a lot of my friends. . . . Everything's been changed.[19]

Eve McNanamy, a clinical psychologist, noticed that as the weeks went by after the hurricane struck, people became very, very anxious. If they were anxious before Hurricane Andrew, they became more anxious after the storm. It they were depressed before, "they certainly became more depressed." She noticed that people began to feel uneasy with the waiting and the uncertainty. The realization that they had lost so much became "appalling, because when you think about it, people lost their homes, they lost their way of life. Many lost their jobs, their neighbors. They've lost the landscape. I've heard so many people mourn the trees, and every day having to see the desolation of an area that was once so rich in foliage is probably the most upsetting for people." She noted that whereas people could rebuild their houses or buy another house, they couldn't replace the very large trees that were gone. Many of her clients lost treasured possessions and memorabilia. Some lost a lifetime of possessions. Others lost friends. High school seniors weren't going to be able to graduate with friends who had moved away. As McNanamy put it, "The losses. There is loss upon loss upon loss."[20]

Some people became angry, but who could they be angry at? The storm? These were the issues and feelings that made it impossible for things to be normal. Even months after the storm, situations arose that once again made it clear that things were not back to normal. McNanamy spoke of a family that had to move in with their parents. Grandparents welcomed their grandchildren, but they also had to find space for their children's sodden and mildewed possessions. Eventually the grandparents wished the children and grandchildren could move out. One of her older clients threatened to commit suicide because he could not take his daughter's family and her children living in his one-bedroom apartment anymore. People were insecure because they did not feel that they could rely on what was the usual way of life—"they no longer have a usual way of life."[21]

Price Gouging

Despite the numerous examples of neighbors helping neighbors after Hurricane Andrew, there were plenty of dark stories about people who decided to take advantage of shortages throughout the county in order to make a profit. In Homestead, ice was being sold for $5 a bag, a $4 increase. A bottle of water was $15. Hotel rooms that normally went for $35 a night suddenly cost $125, and a Denny's restaurant actually charged people $2 just to sit down.[22]

Small scams were commonplace. A few days after Andrew, one of the authors stopped in at the Miami Heroes submarine sandwich shop across from the University of Miami. After ordering his usual $2.95 sandwich, he was presented with a bill for $7. When questioned about the outrageous price, the owner of the shop simply responded that things had changed.

In South Dade, Michael and Greg Reece, who were from Boca Raton, parked their van at the traffic circle where Sunset Drive meets Old Cutler, in the middle of a wealthy neighborhood. The Reeces were selling four-thousand-watt portable generators that they had bought at a Home Depot in Orlando. Michael Reece noticed: "Some people think we're doing a great job, and others think that we're gouging them. For once in our lives, we have something they want. You know these guys are all lawyers and doctors in these neighborhoods, and you know what they charge. So we're here to pinch the people who've never been pinched so they can have their ice cubes."[23]

Sometimes the price gougers got "ripped off" themselves. Metro Dade police officer Jane Jones, who was assigned to the southern end of the county, told a story about "this restaurant down in Cutler Ridge. They have low prices—$4 to $7 type meals. . . . After the hurricane they were loading up trucks with food and selling it off for incredibly high prices. Well, as it turned out, all kinds of people ripped them off. People were angry at them for what they were doing or who needed it . . . I know I'm supposed to be enforcing the law, but I kinda got a laugh, because I'm glad it happened to them rather than to the innocent."[24] Officer Michael Tang recalled

> a gentleman who came all the way from South Carolina with a big truck full of generators. He was selling them for $1500 to $2000. He parked along US 1 and he was not familiar with the area or the neighborhood, not familiar with the delinquents that hang around in that area he was in. He got a gun in his face. They took his truck, his generators, and all his money. [Laughter] It brought happiness to me. We attended to him, we made an effort to look for the truck, because it was wrong and a crime had been committed. However, deep down inside, we were all happy 'cause here was someone who was taking advantage and making profits out of people's misery . . . kind of like, justice was served. It happened backwards, but it worked.[25]

Price gouging is illegal under Florida's Unfair and Deceptive Trade Practices Act.[26] Yet enforcement of the law proved extremely difficult. People often needed services immediately and frequently had no idea what things normally cost. This was certainly the case with services such as tree trimming and in some of the building trades. When Soloman Graham, who works part-time as a landscape and lawn maintenance worker, was asked if he saw price gouging in the landscape business, he responded: "If you're talkin' about clearin' up limbs and trees or somethin' like that, you don't have a book or a scale to go by, so you set your price. And whoever you're settin' your price to, they don't have a scale to go by, so they don't know if it's too much or too less. They need the work done, so if they feel like it's more than what it really is, they're probably still goin' to get you to do the work. So, I would say yes, I see a lot of it."[27]

Rumors Everywhere and Chaos on the Roads

There were times when things seemed to be getting a bit crazy throughout the county. Rumors started popping up everywhere. One story was that large numbers of people had been killed in the southern end of the county. Their bodies were being warehoused by the military and the police in refrigerator trucks. According to another rumor, the 300 monkeys that had escaped from the University of Miami Perrine Primate Center, and the 1,500 monkeys and baboons that had gotten away from the Mannheimer Foundation, were all infected with the AIDS virus. Despite assurances by university and foundation officials that the animals were not carrying the virus, many were shot before they could be recaptured. Of the monkeys from the university's Primate Center, 30 were killed by gunshots, and 15 of the remaining 270 were still unaccounted for a week after the storm.[28]

Things were chaotic on the roads during the first weeks after Hurricane Andrew as well. Most people could not even leave their neighborhoods for several days after the storm because trees and other debris blocked the streets. Sheldon Pivnik, chief of Dade County's Traffic Signals and Signal Division, recalled that the problems faced by his division were unprecedented. In addition to having no power throughout most of the county, and therefore no traffic signals, fallen trees were blocking streets, and vital equipment stored in the southern part of the county had been destroyed in the storm.[29]

Damage to road and highway systems throughout Dade County was extensive. Early estimates put the damage to state roads at between $10 and $20 million. On the Palmetto Expressway, for example, approximately thirty overhead signs were blown away during the storm. By the second anniversary of Andrew, in August 1994, updated figures indicated that signal lights at 2,300 intersections had had to be replaced at a cost of $50 million dollars. More than 50,000 street signs were damaged and had to be replaced, costing about $7.25 million, and 4,600 streetlights were replaced at a cost of $2.3 million.[30]

Metrorail sustained approximately $2 million worth of damage, including the loss of four miles of power rail. In addition, the transit agency lost $600,000 in fares during the first week after the storm because neither buses nor Metrorail trains could run in the county.[31]

Muhammed Mukhtar Hasan, a traffic engineer with the Dade County Public Works Department, was the head of the Traffic Operation and Design Unit at the time of the storm. Essentially, Hasan was responsible for the design of all traffic control devices in the county, including traffic signals and roadway markings. Despite having suffered extensive damage to his house in Kendall and needing to relocate his family to a new home after the storm, Hasan was pressed into service as soon as the storm was over. During the first few days, when virtually all the traffic lights in the county were out because there was no electricity, Hasan found himself directing traffic by hand at Southwest 122nd Avenue and Coral Way.

> Those were the days when the traffic signals were completely out and traffic was really a mess. That was what we did the first couple of days. However, after that, when things started becoming normal, I was put in charge to do the sign inventories for the whole of Dade County. . . . We prioritized. We put all the Stop signs first, and then the second item was the street name signs, because it was difficult for the emergency services and the police to find a particular address to provide the emergency aid. We tried to put the street name signs as the second priority. . . . Traffic signal crews were doing the signal installation, while the sign installation crew was installing Stop signs in the first couple of weeks. To the best of my recollection, so far [as of November 22, 1992], we have installed close to five thousand signs.

During the first weeks following the storm, Hasan and his staff found themselves working twelve-hour shifts, seven days a week. His inventory operation was divided into two phases: "Phase one, we picked up all the area north of North Kendall Drive, and in the second phase of our operation, we picked up the area south of Kendall Drive. . . . Just to give you some sort of an idea as to the damage to the signs, as far as the street name signs are concerned, just for the area north of North Kendall Drive, we will be installing close to ten thousand signs. Probably the number for the area south of Kendall Drive may be much higher than this number."[32]

After the hurricane, volunteers directed traffic at intersections throughout the county. Alexis Martinez, for example, began to direct traffic just a few days after Andrew. Realizing that there was a need, he "called Metro Dade and they informed me that I should call the Red Cross hotline and they might be able to help [find out how and where to volunteer]. . . . They told me to go into the local office and then proceed from there—get an intersection. We were pretty much able to choose an intersection." Martinez received straightforward instructions.

> They just told us to be patient; and they told us pretty much to give traffic the same amount of time in both directions—not to be biased on traffic. They told us to respect the laws or try to apply them a bit, and they told us that people making lefts should go first and people making rights should go second. Basically, just simple little things that you should follow.
>
> Other than that, we were on our own. . . . I volunteered between four and six hours daily. . . . I had to take my own water, my own food. Once in awhile, a cop might pass by the intersection and I might ask him to stay for five or ten minutes so I could go to the restroom or something like that. But other than that, I was on my own.[33]

All that identified Martinez as a traffic director was the fluorescent jacket that the Red Cross had given him to distinguish him from the rest of the civilians in the streets. In the end, volunteer efforts like those of Martinez may have seemed small, but they were critical in reestablishing "normalcy" throughout the county.

Six months after the storm, it was clear that traffic patterns in Dade County had been permanently changed as a result of population relocations. As David Fierro, a local representative for the Florida Department of Transportation, explained: "We're now beginning to see there's going to be a long-term shift. A lot of these people [from South Dade] have relocated, bought a house in Plantation, and they're not coming back." While many people moved elsewhere in the county for housing, their job locations remained the same, causing the rush hour to suddenly expand, stretching from 6:00 to 10:00 A.M. and from 3:00 to 7:00 P.M.. By November 1992, overall traffic in the county had increased 18 percent compared to the same period in 1991.[34]

Meanwhile, in the southern part of the county all the missing street signs still had not been replaced, even by the end of April 1993. According to Metro Dade's Public Works Department, seven thousand intersections were still without signs. Estimates were that it would not be until the end of the summer, a year after the hurricane struck, before all the street signs would be replaced.[35]

The Politics of Hurricane Andrew

The political fallout from Hurricane Andrew was significant at a number of different levels. National figures such as Jesse Jackson appeared in Miami shortly after the storm, calling for minority involvement in the rebuilding process, as well as providing spiritual support to people in the heavily devastated areas. Governor Lawton Chiles visited neighborhood after neighborhood in the first few days after the storm, as did U.S. senators Connie Mack and Bob Graham.

Many of the efforts made by politicians after the storm were, if not heroic, certainly admirable. Otis Wallace, the mayor of Florida City, lost not only his home but also his law practice. Despite these losses, he toured Florida City in the hours and days immediately after the storm, providing consolation and organizing relief efforts wherever he could.[36]

Other politicians failed to deal with the crisis. Dade County mayor Steve Clark did nothing after the storm, remaining holed up in his house in the north part of the county and insisting that directing the relief effort was not his job. Clark's failure to respond to the crisis led Tom Fiedler of the *Miami Herald* to state shortly after the storm that "these past few days and the weeks to come will test the mettle of those to whom we have entrusted our common decisions. We can measure their concern, their competence, maybe even their courage." For Fiedler, Clark's behavior suggested: "Before we punch a ballot we should ask ourselves of the candidates: Can I turn to them in the face of disaster and expect them to be there?"[37] Although Clark's position as Metro mayor was eliminated by court decree before the hurricane struck, it was widely expected that he would run for one of the newly created Metro commission seats. Instead, in late January 1993, he declared that he would not be running for any political office. As many people have said, Hurricane Andrew brought out the best, and the worst, in all of us.[38]

At the state level, involvement with hurricane recovery took place at several different levels. Probably most important, in December 1992 the Florida legislature held a special session to deal with the hurricane. A hurricane relief and recovery fund was established, to be funded from sales taxes during the two years after the storm on items such as building materials and household replacement items. Homestead received $12.8 million of the $16 million it requested, while Florida City received a total of $1.7 million after having asked for $3.2 million. Metro Dade's request from the legislature was for $53 million.[39]

University of Miami president Edward T. Foote II considered the hurricane and the rebuilding process an important moment in the formation of the Miami community:

> The process of the rebuilding effort has been important in terms of redefining leadership in this community. No community can rise above the quality of its own leadership. This is a young, fractured, still developing community. Leadership is one of the key issues in Miami. How does the private sector organize itself to identify the key issues of the time? . . . We haven't done that very well, we really haven't. . . . One of the good things [about the hurricane] is that leaders have come together, people have emerged as leaders. How that plays out, it's too soon to tell, but there's been a lot of good."[40]

Restoring Power and Other Utilities

Whether they were still able to live in their home or were staying with relatives or friends, everyone in the county was affected by the loss of electrical power. Jeffrey Jenkins described how in the week after the storm, he and his family

> had over twenty people living in a three-bedroom, two-bathroom home with no lights or air. Kenny [an AIDS patient] didn't have the

medical equipment he needed. It was hot! But it all boiled down to our family coming together and working together. It was good in that way. We needed that. Doll brought Smokey and Sandra with him. Smokey [a dog] was treated as a human. Smokey had to have his own space. Monkey [Ernest], who doesn't consider himself as being handicapped, was irritable. The babies were crying and the nights were long. But in spite of all this, it brought us closer together. I remember looking at my mom and thinking how strong she was. I thought she was going to break, watching Kenny that first week. She held together, and that made things easier on all of us.[41]

Without electricity and air-conditioning, people found it hard to sleep or to prepare anything approaching a normal meal. Ronald Ponton recalled: "In the evenings were our worst episodes because we had no electricity. So we barbecued every night outside. We had to get charcoal. We had to get ice. We had no electricity for eleven days. Nights were hard sleeping because it was warm outside."[42] Some people slept outdoors on their patio furniture, just to try to escape the heat.

Restoring power after the storm became a major problem for Florida Power and Light. By the weekend after Andrew, approximately 365,000 customers, including 40,000 in Broward County, were still without power. More than two thousand repair workers were brought in from Florida and the Southeast.[43] Repairing downed power lines was complicated by the fact that throughout many parts of the county, scavengers were stealing downed lines and other electrical equipment. Bill Swank, a Florida Power and Light representative, explained: "In some cases, where we could have put back the wire on the pole and restored service right away, we can't because the wire was gone." The theft of supplies from Florida Power and Light compounds after the storm also created problems. More than three thousand pounds of copper wire, for example, was confiscated from a Delray Beach scrap yard. Two men from Palm Beach were arrested for having stolen the wire from a Florida Power and Light compound in Florida City.[44]

A Florida Power and Light employee whose job normally involves working as a liaison between the company and major account holders found himself pressed into fieldwork because of his experience in construction.

As a "utility person," his job after the hurricane was to inspect main feeder lines, subfeeds, and their extension to houses. The crews he worked with were concerned with getting the power back to local neighborhoods and into homes. This was accomplished in a series of stages. As he explained, power was brought in from the local power station, where

> in order to use the transmission line in the local area, you have to step down the voltage. We stepped it down to about 22,000 or 13,000 volts. You can't use that kind of voltage at home! We used that voltage to go down the street. With that amount you can go quite a distance, quite a few customers can be handled with it. When you get to the level of the home, you can handle four or eight customers per home. There is a step further with the transformer, which will bring it down from 22,000 or 13,000 volts to 120, 240, or whatever we use at home.
>
> My function, as well as all the other utility persons, was to inspect the main feeder. Each one of us had one or two feeders assigned to us. We would inspect these from the switchers in the substations all the way down to the end of that feeder. We actually had to get on the street to inspect the feeders in the assigned area and document what we found. [For instance,] was there a tree on the line?

He was initially assigned to work in the Golden Glade area in the north end of town. After a couple of days, he began to work in Carol City and then Liberty City and Overtown. His days working in the field with his crew from out of state were long and hard. "The first day I got home around 10 P.M.. The next day 10 or 11 P.M., it was like from 6:00 A.M. to 10:00 P.M. for the first week or two. Then it began to taper off as time went on to fourteen-hour days, seven days a week. Your body began to get really tired! My son said, 'Dad, when are you going to come home? I miss you.' To me that was the biggest stress, not being able to be home." The issue of safety complicated restoring power in many neighborhoods.

> When it started to turn dark, you needed to start wrapping things up. Because some of the areas in which I was—for example, the Carol City area . . . primarily when we were in the Liberty City and the Overtown area—a neighbor himself told me: "The people here watch out for each other. The daytime they are all right." It was true. . . . So

as it began to turn dark, people began to turn aggressive. If people would not have turned aggressive during the first week, we would have kept on working from 5:30 to 9:30 P.M.[45]

The third week after the hurricane his crew was sent to the southern part of the county to help in repair efforts, he said. "The majority of us were sent down south. I went down to the Redlands. I could see a lot of damage. The concrete transmission poles, which are huge—eight-foot square with rebarbs so many inches apart—these were supposed to withstand two thousand pounds of shear force or the equivalent of 145–mile-hour wind. But the winds far exceeded that. These things were sheared at the bottom like nothing. Some of them were broken in three pieces. Anything that was aluminum—imagine a piece of foil wrapped around a string. That's what it looked like on the lines. In some areas the entire pole lines were sheared at the bottom. They had to do a total overhaul down there, total overhaul." Florida Power and Light had breakfasts and lunches delivered to its workers in the field—approximately sixteen thousand meals were served daily to hurricane restoration workers. Laundry was done daily for more than four thousand employees. For this particular FP&L worker, however, the greatest reward was "hearing the people screaming and shouting for joy" when their power came back on.[46]

Florida Power and Light employees reported working as much as seventy to eighty hours a week. This was all the more remarkable, considering that several thousand of them lived in South Dade and were directly affected by the storm. A total of six hundred families who worked for FP&L had homes so severely damaged that they were uninhabitable. Florida Power and Light tried, as much as possible, to help their employees contact contractors and find the necessary resources to repair their homes. The company had five facilities where their employees could get ice, food, diapers, roofing materials, generators, gas, and just about anything else that they needed.

By September 27, ten days earlier than it had originally projected, Florida Power and Light had restored electrical service to all structures in Dade County capable of receiving it. A total of 620,000 of the company's 820,000 Dade customers had needed to be reconnected after losing their power as a result of Hurricane Andrew.[47]

Andrew also knocked out telephone service for at least 130,000 customers. While most customers in the county had their phone service restored by Southern Bell by the end of October, a number of isolated cases did not regain full service until January 1993. Storer Cable was unable to restore service to all of its customers until early February 1993, but 20,000 Adelphia Cable customers were still without service by mid-February 1993.[48]

Degrees of Homelessness

After Hurricane Andrew, many people had to find housing. More than 10,000 apartments had been destroyed, and owners wanting to undertake repairs on severely damaged structures (more than 13,000) moved people out of their apartments. Almost 9,000 mobile homes had been destroyed, and another 1,000 suffered major damage. More than 8,000 single-family homes had been destroyed, and more than 49,000 had suffered such severe damage that the owners had to move out.

Many people migrated north to Broward County. Paul Dee and his wife, Liz, had nowhere to live. They realized that they needed to have a place where his terminally ill mother-in-law could be with the family, so they moved, within a week, to a house on the Broward/Dade County line. The months after Andrew would prove a difficult time for Dee. While Paul was involved in getting the university open for the new school year, his son and only child was getting ready to begin his first year of college away from home. His mother-in-law passed away just a few months after the storm.

Having lost their home, Suzanne Schorle and her husband decided to pack up their possessions and move out of the area as quickly as possible. A week after the storm, she said, her husband contacted his father and asked him to send a truck down from Pennsylvania. "We started packing. We got boxes from another neighbor who had a pack-n-ship store. . . . And within a week, the moving truck came, and we loaded everything into the moving truck, the entire house. Then we shipped it to Pennsylvania, because that's where we knew people, that's where we had support."[49] Suzanne stayed on in Miami for a few months to sell what remained of her house, but she was gone for good from the South Florida area by the beginning of 1993.

Not everyone was able to find suitable housing, however. A survey of hurricane homeless conducted by government and church workers in early December, a little more than three months after the storm, determined that there were 5,000 people living outdoors in the southern part of Dade County. People were found living in open lots, under tents, and in makeshift shacks. Of the 5,000 people identified, approximately 3,000 were construction workers from out of town; the other 2,000 had been residents of Dade County before the storm. Of these, 800 were children. Nearly all of the 2,000 local residents who found themselves on the street had been evicted from their homes or threatened with eviction.[50]

Some of the homeless were actually drawn to the area by the hurricane. For Salaam Alaikum—homeless and out of work from Pensacola—the relief efforts provided an opportunity for him to receive services that would not otherwise be easily available. Hitchhiking from Pensacola, Alaikum made it to the tent city at Harris Field. He was attracted to Miami by the promise of three free meals a day, a shower, and a bed. As he explained: "I just wanted somewhere to lay my body. Somewhere I could wash. Eat. Somewhere I could be off the ground. Out of the street."[51]

Getting Back to Work

Malcolm Kahn, a psychologist at the University of Miami, was glad to get back to work a week after the storm. It was important to check on colleagues and to make sure that everyone was okay. He was aware of a personal "urgency to try to see if employees needed psychological counseling." Students didn't come back to the university until the third week in September. Kahn noticed that most of the students were able to focus on their studies, but that the staff members who were also students, such as the resident advisors (who were at the university during the storm), were still being affected by the hurricane. Kahn found "that many people want to keep talking about the stress from the aftermath of the storm. This is definitely clouding the attitudes of the staff members and faculty members."[52]

Patricia Whitely also noticed that people at the university were more stressed out, partly because "professors are trying to cram so much into a small semester. . . . This has not been a kinder, gentler semester. They're still trying to do everything they always did." Whitely realized that things were particularly hard for the students who lived in South Dade. Many of them were experiencing family problems. "A lot of [their] options are missing," she noted, partly because there were a lot of places they simply couldn't go."[53]

Grace Laskis, a Head Start disabilities coordinator, tried to find a phone as early as Tuesday, August 25, to see if she should report to work. A message got through to her that she should worry about her personal survival and put work on hold until the next week. Once she felt that there wasn't any more that she could do at home, she said, "I couldn't stay in my house . . . the frustration, the helplessness, was so strong; . . . at least I could go to work and help others . . . and it helped my sanity, getting my routine back." Even though Laskis found that the physical surroundings at work were improving and the buildings were being repaired and services provided, "the psychological part isn't back. We can't concentrate. That emotional unconscious is still there . . . it will be a while before the staff can concentrate like before; . . . it's going to take time, a lot of time."[54]

Michael Laughlin found it hard to have to work during the first week after the storm. He was putting in twelve-hour shifts as a Metro Dade police officer and was unable to work on his house at all. "It was frustrating for my wife to do all the work at the house, and I didn't do anything because by the time I got off work it was time to put the kids down. We had moved into a hotel, so it was very frustrating. As far as work goes, that was also frustrating because I was kept inside the station to do administrative stuff and I wanted to go out and patrol around."[55]

Lauren Markoff had to relocate to a new school, Gilbert L. Porter Elementary. Pine Villa Elementary, where she normally taught, had been badly damaged by the hurricane and further destroyed by looters. She had a long commute to Porter, but the school was so clean and "unharmed" that eventually she liked it. She found that her students were very tired, partly because they had long bus rides to the new school: "Long day with the little ones, they were falling asleep. They were tired and disoriented. . . . We were sharing a classroom. The teachers aren't really all together. They were all badly hurt. Their personal lives destroyed. There has been so much absenteeism. People have their own things to try to pick up and take care of. It affects you indirectly or directly."[56]

LaWanda Scott, a teacher at Canterbury Preschool, found going back to work a relief because it meant that she wouldn't have to cope with the stress at home. "I wouldn't have to deal with a lot of things . . . being here relieves my mind. This is like my escape. . . . When I am home, it is just too much." Even though the children provided temporary distraction, Scott was very much aware that she was walking around in a daze.[57]

Survivor Guilt and Victim Resentment

An interesting aspect of Hurricane Andrew that was not often discussed was the guilt felt by many people who were less affected by the storm than were other members of their family or their friends. Sometimes it was hard to talk to colleagues and friends who had been much more profoundly affected. James Mooney explained the guilt he felt when he left the devastation surrounding his job and many of his colleagues to return to his relatively undamaged home in the northern part of the county. For a very long time, he said, he felt that "I shouldn't be going home to air-conditioning, and I had a structure that was standing and not leaking, and that my friends and colleagues were going home to a lean-to kind of environment." Mooney also found himself needing to "develop a kind of sensitivity to what staff was experiencing . . . to try to understand . . . to try to be flexible in terms of work schedule, demands, and expectations on the staff."[58]

Pat Ashley was particularly sensitive to the many levels and types of suffering that people experienced in the community. "Another kind of awareness for me [after the hurricane] is that there are all kinds of suffering, and whatever kind of suffering somebody is in is valid. I've had so many people say, 'We're not starving to death, we're not at the level of devastation as those in the Homestead area.' But the upheaval in people's lives, the personal turmoil of having every routine and every self-understanding turned upside down, is also suffering."[59]

Those who were more directly affected often unconsciously ostracized those who had suffered less physical damage. Claudia Shukat, an insurance claims manager, who got through the storm with relatively little damage to her home, explained how some people she was helping to file claims would talk to her. "'You're sitting here . . . your house wasn't damaged, you have no understanding for what I'm going through.' What kind of an argument is that? You know I'm sitting there grateful that my house wasn't damaged, but it is nothing that I did to deserve it. It is nothing that you did to deserve that yours got blown away." In fact, Shukat, while not an apparent victim, was under abnormal stress for weeks, if not months, following the hurricane.

> My life has become a ten- to twelve-hour workday, more or less . . . an all-consuming type of thing. The first six to eight weeks it was next to impossible to shut it out of your leisure time . . . because you are so high-strung and so caught up in it with all the extra work, the extra worry, the extra responsibility, the extra aggravations. You simply can't shut it off by the time you get home. And I am still working long hours. The mood has changed somewhat. We have become very resigned to the fact that this is not going to have a happy ending, and the effect on my personal life is still a daily effect that everybody in the family gets to feel.[60]

Sometimes people who had suffered less damage from Hurricane Andrew were treated with disdain by those who had been more hard hit. Throughout the interviews conducted for this study, over and over again people expressed the conviction that no one could really understand the enormity of the storm unless they lived south of 152nd Street. Sharon Johnson, for example, recounted that she gets "irritated by people who think they suffered and really didn't . . . people in Kendall who maybe didn't really have it that bad but kind of thought that they did. But, you know, it's like their experience was their experience . . . they can't know what it was like for other people. . . . In my mind, south of Coral Reef Drive is where it really starts getting bad . . . south of 152nd . . . that's the line for me."[61] Johnson's house was at 196th Street, one block west of Old Cutler. Ironically, we heard people much farther south in Homestead and Florida City who maintained that people in Johnson's neighborhood really hadn't suffered that much in the storm.

Irene Baljet, who had weathered Andrew at a distance, considered herself to have gone through a unique type of pain and distress.

A lot of people say to me, "Oh, you were so lucky you were not here." I totally disagree with that because, number one, you feel the guilt for not being here and helping to tie down the house. Here I was in a hotel, air-conditioned, having a nice meal, and my husband is out for fourteen hours straight putting up shutters. My daughter is carrying in all my plants. And when it happens, you are not there to either comfort them—the comfort that comes from all being together—or do the physical work that needed to be done. . . . I don't consider myself lucky.[62]

Perhaps the point should not be who suffered more, but the extent to which the entire community went through the trauma of Hurricane Andrew. Everyone was vulnerable. As Pat Ashley noted, even people with financial means were still helpless. "It was the helplessness more than the patch on the roof that needed to be addressed. If you couldn't find a person to fix your roof . . . a million dollars didn't help one bit."[63]

This trauma was not limited to surviving the hurricane but included the process of rebuilding the community. The scope and magnitude of this process started to become clear in the weeks and months after the storm. Hurricane Andrew was a collective experience. It affected everybody's life. It was in every conversation. Almost everyone in Dade County had to begin to rebuild their lives.

Rebuilding the Community

6

After a disaster like Hurricane Andrew, there comes a point when people are ready to try to get beyond dealing with the immediate crisis and to think about the future. Many in Dade County had reached this point about four weeks after the storm struck, when the Hurricane Relief Concert organized by Gloria and Emilio Estefan was held.

While some community leaders stayed away from the areas of Dade County most devastated by the hurricane, cool and safe in their air-conditioned homes, Gloria and Emilio Estefan were there for the community from the beginning. They went to Homestead, bringing with them sup-

A 1-by-4 board driven through the trunk of a royal palm by Hurricane Andrew. (Image ID: wea00546)

plies and smiles. They gave cash donations. And they helped get Hurricane Andrew Relief off the ground, including the Hurricane Relief Concert. The concert, starring Gloria Estefan, Paul Simon, Celia Cruz, and Jimmy Buffett, was held at Joe Robbie Stadium in North Dade and raised $1.3 million from sales of $10, $25, and $100 tickets—52,000 tickets. Concertgoers were advised to arrive early—as early as 3:30 P.M., well before the warm-up band began at 5:00.[1]

Gabriel Gabor, marketing manager for the James L. Knight Center, got to the stadium at 8:00 A.M.. He could have stayed at home in the air-conditioning, but he chose not to. Gabor had spent the night that Hurricane Andrew struck in the honeymoon suite at the Quality Inn near the airport, together with his father, mother, stepmother, baby sister and her babysitter, and his best friend. They had gone to the motel because they lived in an evacuation zone. Safely settled in, surrounded by a hot tub, a big-screen TV, and lounge couches, Gabor said his biggest concern had been whether his sister would be scared by the noise of the storm.

The motel turned out to be a good place to weather the storm. Winds and damage in the area around the airport were far less severe than even a few miles farther south. Gabor stayed at his mother's for the first week after Andrew, since his electricity was off and her apartment building had its own generator. At his mother's, Gabor "had electricity, cable, telephone, and everything else from day one, so I stayed there the first week. I didn't go to work, and I was—I was having a very different experience than most people in the county." Gabor spent a lot of time watching TV at his mother's and heard the reports about all the different volunteer efforts. "It was frustrating, 'cause as much as I wanted to volunteer, . . . on the news [they said], 'Don't go, they have enough volunteers.'"[2]

Feeling that he needed to contribute to the recovery, Gabor jumped at the chance to help when he heard that Gloria and Emilio Estefan wanted to put on a Hurricane Relief Concert. He was given the job of checking the credentials of more than five hundred media people and of handing out press passes. His shift was over at noon, but Gabriel stayed on, helping with the press and interviews until 3:30 in the morning. "Everybody that was in the stadium that wasn't attending [the concert] was a volunteer. Every performer was a volunteer. Every journalist was a volunteer." At the stadium, Gabriel said, he overheard many stories from those attending the concert "because, you know, they just went through the worst hell you can imagine . . . they are all coming out, spending twenty-five to a hundred bucks a person . . . to sit for six hours in a concert and listen to music. I think that after four weeks of hell, everybody needed a picker-upper."[3]

The Disabled and Hurricane Andrew

Hurricane Andrew exacted a particularly heavy toll on disabled members of the South Florida community. The failure of electrical power throughout the area meant that electric wheelchairs could not be recharged, telephones specially designed for use by the deaf could not be used, and special services that were normally accessible to the disabled were no longer available. Emergency facilities such as the tent city in Homestead found it extremely difficult to serve individuals with special needs. Saribel Ceballos, a nurse at the Debbie School—a special-education center based at the University of Miami Medical School—recalled significant numbers of children "in Tent City, handicapped in wheelchairs, with aerosol treatments, oxygen dependent—real heavy duty. We had one kid . . . who was on O_2 [oxygen dependent all day], and he was in Tent City for a while. Somehow they connected him to a generator, and it was a big deal with the mom."[4]

Twelve group homes clustered in the Goulds area and run by Miami Cerebral Palsy were destroyed by the storm. The ninety-six clients living in the homes, who lost almost all their personal possessions, had to be relocated to temporary facilities in the Pembroke Pines Hospital. Many of those who were moved because of the storm, and who were normally able to feed themselves, use the bathroom, and dress themselves, could no longer do so in the first weeks and months following the storm because they had lost their mechanical support systems.[5] In addition to the loss of their facility, many of the people who had worked in the group homes in South Dade quit their jobs after Andrew. Of the 325 United Cerebral Palsy workers responsible for the residents before the storm, 200 quit after the hurricane. As a result, new workers had to be trained and assigned to work with patients who were already severely stressed because of the storm and the move to a new facility.[6]

At the Debbie School, part of the University of Miami Jackson Memorial Hospital, which provides services for mentally, physically, and emotionally challenged children throughout the county, normal school schedules were totally disrupted by the storm. Blake Bergman, a teacher in a special program associated with the Debbie School, recalled that the hurricane required that extraordinary measures be taken with many of the children he worked with who were connected to heart monitors or tracheal tubes and needed access to emergency power. In addition, ten new children arrived at the school because their foster parents had lost their homes or their shelters were destroyed during the hurricane. Three of the nurses Bergman worked with had also lost their homes. One of them was going to move out of the area; the second could no longer work full-time; and he felt the third was close to having a nervous breakdown.[7]

The training schedules of the children under Bergman's care had been entirely disrupted. He explained that they had to start over again from scratch, training the children to feed themselves, to drink from a cup, even to walk.[8] A job as difficult and complex as dealing with children with special physical needs had become even more complicated as a result of Hurricane Andrew.

Social Service and Support Workers

One of the most important aspects of Hurricane Andrew was that it affected the entire community. Its victims included those who were expected to provide social and recovery services. As a result, besides having to cope with their own recovery problems, they had to handle the additional issue of burnout. As James White, a counseling psychologist, explained: "I got burnt out, burnt out from the standpoint of a therapist, of being in one of the worst positions you can be in—therapeutic despair. Therapeutic despair is a way of saying . . . you work so hard with a person that you don't see results . . . you don't seem to be making ground. . . . I was looking forward many times just to going home, not turning on the TV, listening to music, and just kind of meditating." Among his co-workers, White noted: "There's numbness, particularly with my colleagues . . . those that were directly affected [or] indirectly, through family members, cousins, relatives, friends. There's numbness. There's sadness. There's hope, but there's so much pain. . . . You can see it on their faces: 'Where do I go now? What am I going to do?' 'I've gotta go to work, but I also have to go and take care of this?' 'Are they going to loot what's remaining in my home?'"[9]

James Mooney said that among his counseling staff at Metro Dade's Department of Youth and Family Development in the southern half of the county, approximately 25 percent lost their homes or had major devastation. Many of his staff "had experienced equal or worse devastation than the clients we service, so we really were running kind of two tracks—one was to serve our own staff and their immediate needs, and the other was to serve our clients." Mooney felt that it was imperative that his staff receive personal support in working through their own problems and stresses, even while they were serving their clients.[10]

Red Cross administrator Lawrence Moose also was aware that social service workers often felt overwhelmed by the magnitude of the storm. Many of them were upset with their inability to meet the needs of the people they were supposed to serve.

> It was really frustrating the first week or so. . . . You know, it was so big, what do you do first? We have a lot of people with experience, but who has experience [with] a . . . catastrophic disaster? . . . I know the feeling of helplessness that the agency felt [the Red Cross], and I think Dade County Emergency Management felt, and some of the other agencies felt . . . in not having the resources, not being able to immediately respond to the vast sea of needs that were out there. And just feeling like we are here to do this, and we are willing to do it, but we don't have the staff, the material, the access, all these things. . . .
>
> The hours go by, and you are thinking, "Gosh, if I could just be on the road," but you can't make it through on the road. Knowing that people need food and not being able to get it to them—tough situation to be in.[11]

The Impact on the Environment

Hurricane Andrew created a severe strain not only on the people of South Florida, but also on the environment. By the first week of September, thirty trash-burning sites had been set up across the county. Everything from tree branches to asphalt roofing shingles, furniture, and other debris was being disposed of at the burning sites. Environmentalists were particularly concerned about potential toxins from items such as plastics and asphalt being released into the air. In addition, there was concern that ash from the burning would eventually seep into the area's groundwater supply.[12]

Harold Wanless, associate professor of geology at the University of Miami and an expert on coastal ecology and geology, noted that the long-term environment and ecology of an area often get overlooked when a disaster like Hurricane Andrew strikes—people are so busy coping with the immediate crisis.

> In a catastrophe like this, we get so overwhelmed with human tragedy that you forget the environment. You ignore making sure that the people [who] should be looking at the evidence for the currents, or the evidence of the waves, or the evidence for the pollution—that really has to be done right away. There must be a mechanism set up to make that happen. The State Department of Natural Resources was driving down Sunday night . . . and Monday afternoon they were measuring beach profiles. They were the only organization that I saw that mobilized the instantaneous scientific response and monitoring.[13]

For scientists interested in coastal ecology, Hurricane Andrew represented an interesting phenomenon. According to Wanless: "Usually, if you have a storm with 170- or 200–mile-an-hour winds, you have it move across and spend three to ten, twelve, hours lashing at a shoreline. And you have this horrendous erosion and modification. Huge inlets form. What we saw was the incipient stages of overwash from the very strong storm surges, and the channeling that starts to form with it. We saw channeling start to dissect mangrove coastlines." The hurricane was the beginning of an experiment in redefining Southeast Florida's coastal ecology, according to Wanless. As a scientist, he considered Hurricane Andrew a wonderful storm. "There's stuff I never conceived would happen. Like gravel filling mailboxes west of Homestead. Gravel from the fields and not somebody's roof. And gravel being imbedded up to sixteen or more feet in pine trees. Somebody just gave me a photograph that a plumber had taken down around 248th Street, where there's a 2 x 4 stuck right through a palm tree. You hear about these things in dust storms and tornadoes. But to see these things as part of a hurricane is phenomenal."[14]

According to Wanless, the destruction caused by the hurricane also provided an interesting opportunity to correct earlier ecological mistakes. For example, in the case of Cape Florida Park, "over 90 percent of the Australian pines went down. They're going to redesign the park as a natural system. Cape Florida is a park, but it was 'fill' in the fifties and it grew up with Australian pines. They just sort of took over. So when it became a park in the late sixties, it was an Australian pine park. Now is an opportunity for it to revert to a natural setting."[15]

Hurricane Andrew cut a twenty-mile swath across 1.5 million acres of Everglades National Park. Although park facilities were severely damaged, the main concern was that the seeds of pest plants such as the Brazilian pepper and the Australian malaleuca would spread. Wanless explained how pest plants or "exotics" spread as a result of the storm:

> The diameter of the storm was approximately twelve miles—let's say fifteen miles, . . . the circumference of the inner wall about fifty miles. Let's say the storm has 150–miles-per-hour winds. That means that every hour your particle would go around three times. . . . Florida is roughly ninety miles across, and it [the storm] went across in three hours. So let's say the front edge of this inner eyewall picked up something, a bunch of it, and it mixed it up in the storm. Every hour it went around three times, so that pollen could have been spun around nine times as it went across the state.[16]

In addition, rotting debris choked the estuaries, which were vital nurseries for fish. The hurricane destroyed rookeries for wading birds. Mangroves, hardwood hammocks, and stands of slash pines were also severely damaged.[17]

The failure to fully document the storm—its wind speeds, weather conditions, and so on—was a particular disappointment for scientists such as Wanless. "The government tragedy is that in the day of sending probes to Mars, we have no idea what the bloody winds were in this storm. We don't know the barometric pressure, we don't know the winds, and we don't know the currents that were generated out in the coastal environment. I fail to understand how we can protect and build for the future. This is the biggest natural disaster in U.S. history." According to Wanless, the failure to collect accurate wind speeds during the storm was "a horrible tragedy to the future of humanity that's going to build houses in the coastal zone, where winds are going to get at them. I mean, this storm was a lesson in winds, and we don't know what the lesson was." Wanless fears that, "in a year, people are going to start to forget everything, and people are going to let building codes slip a little bit. Every year it'll slip a little bit more. And fifteen years from now, we'll have forgotten most of the things that everybody in Dade County has learned from this storm. It's amazing how rapidly we forget."[18]

The destruction caused by Hurricane Andrew to the $150 million nursery and foliage industry in Dade County was enormous. Most of the $20 million lime crop was uprooted by the storm. Only part of the $13 million avocado crop had been harvested before the storm. Nearly all of the packinghouses in the southern part of the county were destroyed. According to Florida commissioner of agriculture Bob Crawford, the 7,200–acre nursery industry was almost completely wiped out.[19]

Pablo E. Perez is the owner of the Rain Forest Nursery located just north of Homestead that was severely affected by the storm. Like many others throughout the county, Perez thought that the storm would probably bypass Miami. As a nursery owner he had dealt with bad weather and freezes before, but nothing like Hurricane Andrew. When he came out of his home after Andrew and was finally able to make it back to the nursery, he saw an unprecedented level of destruction. While he described having "been through a lot of natural acts of God before," what he now saw before him was "stunning."[20]

In many respects, according to Perez, the hurricane was much more difficult to defend against than a freeze. In the case of a freeze, there are several methods of preparing, but "in a hurricane like this you don't know from which direction the winds are coming. There is not much you can do with a hurricane. . . . What you can do is think after the fact. You can think, 'What can I do now to make our rebuilding process easier and try to save as much as possible from damage?'"[21] Foliage plants, normally grown in shade houses that were destroyed, died within two or three days because they were suddenly exposed to direct sunlight. Trees that were blown over could survive for a couple of weeks but had to be righted reasonably quickly or they would suffer permanent damage.

At Perez's nursery, which specialized in woody ornamental plants, the damage caused by the hurricane was not as serious as that for the foliage nursery growers. Most of Perez's plants were grown in containers that could be put upright again after they were blown over. In addition, Perez did not suffer from salt-water intrusion from the ocean, which had happened to many of the nurseries farther south.

Tony Costa's Costa Nursery Farms was much more directly affected by the storm. At Costa's family-owned business, which employs 450 people, Andrew destroyed 95 percent of the plants. Costa estimated his losses at between $15 and $20 million. As is typical in the industry, only his buildings, not his plants, were insured. Nonetheless, Costa was somewhat fortunate, since a large part of his operation is in Haiti and the Dominican Republic.[22]

Overall, Hurricane Andrew caused $1.04 billion in damage to the agricultural community in South Florida. Next to the Grain Belt drought in 1988, it was the most costly agricultural disaster in the country's history. Compared to South Florida's Christmas freeze of 1989, when losses were estimated at $500 million, Hurricane Andrew was twice as costly.[23]

In the weeks and months following the storm, pest control became a major problem in South Dade. Mounds of storm debris that accumulated as a result of the storm provided ideal breeding grounds for rats. With the growth of the rat population, snakes that feed on rats grew in number as well, including Everglades Racers, Corn Snakes, Yellow Rat Snakes, and Everglades Rat Snakes.[24]

Animals such as 'possums and raccoons were displaced by the storm, along with human beings. After the hurricane was over, these animals found shelter in abandoned homes and buildings. Richard Anderson, a technician with Truly Nolen Pest Control assigned to South Dade, explained:

> The biggest problem we had was so many homes were no longer a sealed unit, with roof damage or walls blown in, or cracks around windows and door frames. It makes it very difficult to control for pests when you don't have a sealed environment. You can do all you want to inside a house, but if holes still exist for passage, it is tough to control. You really have to do a good exterior spray around a house to keep insects from getting into the house to begin with. That is the primary thing—the outside barrier—from getting into the house. That was really hard to control at first because of the damage to homes.

Prior to the storm, Anderson's work mostly involved spraying insecticides to control small sugar ants and roaches. After the storm, ants and roaches proliferated throughout the area. In addition: "We also started getting many calls about mice and rats that were run out of their homes because of the downed trees. A lot more activity was seen after the storm because of all the tree damage, because that is where many of the insects live. So everything we saw was just accelerated." It is interesting to note that according to Anderson, there were widespread reports of insect activity immediately before Hurricane Andrew, as well. "People saw swarming of certain types of insects prior to the storm where they mated, paired up, and went back into the structures of the walls. . . . The ants come out, they pair up to mate, and they go back and start a new colony. This is what we found them doing, as if they understood there was going to be something happening to take away from their population, so in an effort to save that, they increased."[25]

In addition to the problem of bugs and other animals after Hurricane Andrew, mold became a major issue. Karen Baldwin recalled that a little more than a week after the storm, when water was finally restored, she began to scrub down the walls of her house to get rid of the mold and mildew that had accumulated. However, the mold and mildew refused to stop growing back.

You went through, you cleaned as much of walls as you can get to ... and you think that things are looking pretty good. "Hey, now I can put things away." And you get up the very next morning and you've got brand-new mold and mildew all over everything again. It's just an endless cycle. Redo it and redo it. As you're walking around the house and you start pulling things out—because we've literally pulled everything out of every drawer, every closet—in an attempt to get them outside and dried out. And all of a sudden you open a drawer to ... take out a telephone book, and you look at the telephone book and it's got mold and mildew growing on it. The reason is that it's sitting in a puddle—a half inch of water in the drawer.

Every time you turn a corner, you find something else that has been destroyed by the wind, by the original water, or by the creeping mold and mildew. Sometimes the feeling is there—you almost think—"Would it not have been better for the whole thing to have just blown away and start totally from scratch, than having to fight this on a day-to-day basis, of trying to keep things *clean*?"[26]

Metrozoo and Other Tourist Attractions

Many of the county's major tourist attractions were hit hard by the storm, including Metrozoo, Parrot Jungle, Monkey Jungle, and the Miami Seaquarium. Total damage to public parks in the area was placed at $80 million.[27] Monkey Jungle, a twenty-five-acre tourist attraction and primate behavior research facility located in the southern end of the county, sustained approximately $2 million in damage.[28] According to John Frosbutter, manager of Bill Baggs Cape Florida State Park, more than three hundred acres at the park on Key Biscayne were leveled by the high winds.[29] Parrot Jungle, a popular aviary and garden complex, reopened September 14. Attractions such as the Barnacle Historical Museum, the Charles Deering Estate, and Everglades National Park were closed throughout the fall.[30]

The Miami Seaquarium was closed until December 15. Before the storm, careful plans had been formulated on how to deal with a hurricane. As Richard B. Howard, executive vice-president of the Seaquarium, explained, the hurricane plan is "like general quarters on a ship. Everybody knows what their assignments are and what they're supposed to do as we go to the next-closer warning that triggers the next series of things to do. . . . It deals with everything from putting in extra animal food located on the mainland, because we don't know what circumstances will be here, and lots of little things."[31] Andrew Feldman, who worked at Miami Seaquarium, recalls going back to work three days after the storm and finding the conditions "gross." While the storm had not destroyed any buildings, all the sharks in the shark channel had been killed because of problems with the filtration pumps. In addition, five sea lions had been accidentally electrocuted.[32]

Hurricane Andrew more seriously affected the Metrozoo than any of the other major tourist attractions in the county. The zoo was in the direct path of the storm and winds estimated at more than two hundred miles per hour.[33] Although relatively few large animals were killed by the storm—one impala, one onager, one Grimm's duiker, one dik-dik, one ostrich, and a baby gibbon—the aviary was destroyed and 120 birds either were killed or flew away in the storm.[34] The animal food preparation facilities were destroyed and food supplies spoiled. The diagnostic lab and its lifesaving facility were destroyed. The education building and all its equipment and records were in ruins. The gift shop, the Koala exhibit, the children's zoo, the amphitheater, the warehouse, animal night houses, breeding facilities, quarantine facilities, vehicles, gates, and even the perimeter fence were destroyed or damaged.[35]

Damien Kong, a Metrozoo zoologist who worked in the education department, described how the zoo's staff had tried to prepare for Hurricane Andrew. "They secured all the animals that they thought could get blown away. They put all the animals in their night houses, in the back areas, so we did as much as we could." Eight zoo workers spent the night of the hurricane in the animal hospital cages with birds, a Key deer, a baby gerenuk, and several duikers. Kong described the destruction immediately after the storm as "just overwhelming. There were trees down everywhere. Buildings were damaged. Roads were blocked. A lot of the roads had trees and rocks all over the roads that you couldn't drive. In other words, it was very hard to get in certain sections of the zoo." Kong's wife, a zookeeper, came home the day after the storm and "just cried and cried," Kong said.

Projects that had been under development for years were "now gone or put on hold. One of our major projects that we had coming up was something called the South American Rain Forest Exhibit. We had already raised a few million dollars to build that, and it's not even going to be getting off the ground. Some of the money was earmarked. That means that the money was donated specifically for that exhibit. That means that we can't use it for rebuilding the zoo."[36]

Besides the destruction to the zoo's facilities, there was the possibility that if the zoo did not reopen soon, its employees would lose their jobs. In fact, many of the people who worked with the private arm of the zoo—the Zoological Society—rather than for the county did lose their jobs. As Kong explained: "With the Zoological Society, only sixteen people regained their jobs out of forty-one. So with the zoo not being open, it's hard to keep a lot of people on. I mean, I was worried for about a month. Even right now, the nature of my job has changed. I'm not in education anymore. I'm a zoologist by degree. . . . And now I'm in fund-raising until we resurrect the zoology department. Because we have to get the zoo going before any other kind of program can get going."[37]

After the storm, large numbers of volunteers showed up at the zoo to help with the cleanup. Animals were shipped off to temporary homes at other zoos, Kong said. "Most of the birds at the zoo have been shipped out. A lot of the birds were recaptured from the aviary, for instance, but none of the birds were kept. They were shipped immediately to other facilities. We have birds all of the way up to Nebraska."[38]

One of the people killed by Hurricane Andrew was twelve-year-old Naomi Browning. Before the storm, Naomi was a zoo volunteer who had been selected to assist Damien Kong with animals in the classroom. Kong remembered her as "a good kid. She had lots of initiative and was very focused. She wasn't afraid of anything, not insects, not cleaning up after the animals." Naomi, said Kong, was a "true animal person." During the hurricane, Naomi's mother recalled that her daughter was more worried about the animals than her own danger. On December 5, 1992, the white tiger exhibit at the zoo was rededicated as the Naomi Browning Tiger Temple, in her memory and to honor all children who love the zoo.[39]

Metrozoo finally reopened on December 18—four months after Hurricane Andrew struck South Florida. Approximately 1,800 people came for the reopening, twice the normal daily attendance. Many of the animals were skittish, hiding behind trees and rockwork. Exhibits such as the koalas, Asian elephants, and aviary remained closed, along with the monorail. The park, which had been heavily planted with trees before the storm, was barren—between five and six thousand trees had been destroyed by the hurricane.[40]

Attendance at South Florida tourist attractions like Metrozoo was seriously affected by the storm. By the end of January 1993, Metrozoo's attendance was down by one-half. At Fairchild Tropical Garden, attendance had declined by 62 percent, while Everglades National Park's visitors were down by 40 percent and Villa Vizcaya's by 35 percent. Under normal circumstances, about half the visitors to South Florida's tourist attractions are from the local area. With their time taken up trying to repair damage after the storm, many South Florida residents did not find themselves with the leisure to visit tourist attractions. As Metrozoo director Bob Yokel explained, "If you have any spare time, you're dealing with a contractor and a roofer and an insurance company, or you're out shopping for a new refrigerator or a new washer-dryer."[41]

Retail Sales

Retailers both large and small in the southern part of the county were devastated as a result of Hurricane Andrew. The Burdines Department Store in Cutler Ridge Mall sustained $15 million in damages. Considerable speculation in the first months after the hurricane focused on whether or not malls such as Cutler Ridge would eventually reopen. Bloomingdale's in the Falls Shopping Center was scheduled to reopen in November, but as a result of construction related to a fire, the opening was postponed. Lurias, a local appliance and jewelry chain, scheduled its Suniland Shopping Center location to reopen by November 1, while the Cutler Ridge location was slated for reopening at some indefinite time in the future.[42]

For many retail outlets the hurricane proved an incredible boon. As a result of the storm, South Dade became the most active retail furniture market in the country. Cynthia Cohen Turk, a Miami retail analyst, estimated that Dade County would see approximately $500 million spent on replacement furniture as a result of Hurricane Andrew. Typical of Andrew victims needing replacement furniture was Ginger Parker, a Miami-Dade Community College professor, whose East Perrine home was destroyed by the storm. According to Parker: "Everything was destroyed, everything. I need tables, chairs, beds, couches—the works. I've got insurance money to pay for it, too."[43]

Several of the large retail furniture stores in the area, such as Levitz Furniture, Modernage, and Rhodes, suffered major storm damage. Levitz Furniture's 180,000–square-foot showroom on Quail Roost Drive was totally destroyed. Companies such as Carl's Furniture and Baer's Furniture opened new stores in the area, hoping to capitalize on the huge replacement market that developed after the storm.[44]

The Insurance Crisis

By the second anniversary of Hurricane Andrew, 795,912 insurance claims had been filed, with $16.04 billion in claims paid. The average claim was $20,162.[45] The storm precipitated an insurance crisis throughout the South Florida community. After the storm, five small insurance companies went bankrupt, stranding sixteen thousand policyholders in South Dade.[46] The Florida Insurance Guaranty Association (FIGA) guaranteed the policies for the bankrupt companies. The FIGA, however, was seriously underfunded. It had less than $50 million set aside, while anticipated losses from Hurricane Andrew were $450 million.

A 2 percent levy on premiums collected from policyholders throughout the state—which was allowed under existing law—would raise only $70 million. Tom Gallagher, the state insurance commissioner, proposed selling tax-exempt bonds through the City of Homestead that would be used to raise the additional $400–$500 million needed by the FICA to pay off the policyholders of bankrupt insurance companies.[47] For people who had lost their homes and then found out that their insurance companies were bankrupt, the situation was particularly difficult. Not only did they have to go through the red tape of recovering their losses through the state fund, but also they had to go out on the open market to get new insurance.

As Claudia Shukat, an insurance claims manager with Nova Southern, explained: "If the company is put into liquidation, then the in-force policies get a thirty-day cancellation from the date the order is entered. The policyholders have to fend for themselves, which of course is going to be next to impossible for homeowners, because there aren't too many companies that are willing to take on homeowners that they haven't insured in the past. And that brings us back to the state, because the state will then have to offer a six-months policy JUA [Joint Underwriters Association] type program, a risk pool." Shukat accurately predicted that, after Hurricane Andrew, insurance companies would increase their premiums in Florida. She also believed that they would try to limit their financial exposure in the future by cutting back on storm coverage:

> It's quite, quite apparent that not only will premiums go up but also companies are trying to limit their exposure in Florida. They are doing it already. Big companies, State Farm. . . . They are reunderwriting existing policies, and they are looking at everything very carefully. They are limiting the amount of new premium, new policies that can be written in that particular area. Everybody is taking a hit. Small companies are going out of business simply because all their financial surplus that backs up the normal operations in claims paying is going out for [the] hurricane. There is nothing left.[48]

The impact of the storm on individual companies like Shukat's was enormous. In addition to the company's being seriously understaffed, claims were being placed against it by huge numbers of their policyholders:

> It has been a nightmare really. . . . We've had people transfer from other departments to the claim department because we didn't have the manpower to handle it. We've had to bring in an outside adjuster, an adjuster-for-hire, so to speak, who works with us in the office. Because we can't hire a permanent person, we have had to do it on a temporary basis. And the outgoing claims payments have pretty well reduced the surplus of the company to zilch. The company is no longer able to write any policies. People have been laid off, and sooner or later—probably sooner, rather than later—there won't be any more Nova Southern. It's just a matter of a couple more weeks. . . .

Whatever homeowners' policies we had in force in the Homestead, Leisure City, South Miami area past Kendall, was 100 percent claim incident. Every last policy has a claim. From there on up . . . I would say it is about 70 percent of those going up to maybe Flagler Street. And then you have Hialeah, where the storm must have been immensely intense, because just about 80 percent of our policies there . . . have made claims. And there's certain pockets where—I guess it's the densely populated areas—where once one person makes a claim and gets money out of it, it's contagious.[49]

In addition to the enormous damages actually sustained, insurance companies also had to contend with inflated costs from contractors for both supplies and labor:

I'm not for a minute doubting the validity of damage. What is bringing it down [the insurance business] is the amount being charged to repair. The Insurance Department got in on this from a fairly early point. When they realized the contractors were adjusting to the supply-and-demand theory and hiking their prices, doubling their prices, they tried to put out guidelines. They'll say: "You're supposed to pay based on these guidelines, pricing guidelines"—largely prestorm guidelines with minor adjustments.

And the contractors got together and put up a tremendous fight and three weeks later the guidelines were revised to reflect what the contractors were charging, which were at least twice what were there before. Sometimes more. The longer people are waiting and arguing, the tougher it is to find a contractor. . . . I've spoken to adjusters who themselves were involved in the area that got hit and have extensive damage in their homes and have found it firsthand with people they have dealt with over the years [who] are no longer dealing on the same level. They're trying to get a contract price paid by the [insurance] company that is way, way inflated, and then they are trying to subcontract it out for a great deal less and are trying to line their pockets.[50]

Pressures on local agents to meet claims were enormous. Shukat explained that she "had about 1,280 claims from the hurricane. . . . We normally . . . get 60 or 70 a month. So it's two years' worth of claims in three months. And this is a company that's not geared to that. You still have to keep track of the money you spend, you have to keep track of the paperwork, you have to report to the Department [state insurance], to your owners, to everybody, to your re-insurers. . . . I have some very dedicated people in the claim department who are working themselves into little pieces of nervous balls." Stress for claimants and the pressure placed on insurance adjusters was enormous, with even racial issues coming into play.

It is being made into not only something personal, but you get the racial factor involved. People are sitting there saying, "Well, you are only not paying me because I'm black." Now this is such an incredibly ludicrous thing to say, but people are so frustrated . . . that [they'll do] everything that they can think of to try to force you into doing something right now. . . . People are being very unreasonable. I've had plenty of people call me later and apologize. And you have got to understand that the stress is horrendous on everybody. And I do have a great deal of sympathy for everybody who was really, really affected. And these people's lives are a far cry from being back to normal.[51]

Cheating on Insurance and Other Scams

In the weeks and months after the storm, there were numerous stories throughout the community about people who benefited from the storm by cheating on their insurance. Juan Hernandez (a pseudonym), who lives in Hialeah, thought that the effect of the storm in his own life was "great," since it gave him the opportunity to file false insurance claims and remodel his house. Although the storm was a frightening experience for Hernandez and his family, they suffered relatively little damage compared to most people. "A window broke. There was a shingle that broke the window and water started coming in. Luckily we had a piece of sheet rock and that is what we covered the window with. Basically that is all that happened to our house." No more than ten ceramic roof tiles had been blown off Hernandez's house by the hurricane. Following the storm, however, Hernandez used a hammer to smash a large number of tiles so that he could collect more insurance. In addition, he lined up trees that had been cut before the hurricane so that it appeared that they had fallen onto his roof and deck as a result of the storm. "I just gave them a better push and they fell right on top of the wood deck," Hernandez said.[52]

Hernandez did not tell his wife or his family that he was falsifying damages to his house. According to him, his actual damages were about $2,000, but he was able to collect $25,000. With the money that he received from his insurance company, Hernandez upgraded his house. He rationalized that he had been paying insurance premiums for years and that the hurricane was "an opportunity to upgrade or help a lot of poor people who didn't have enough money to upgrade their house."[53]

Following the storm, insurance fraud also occurred on a much smaller and less overt scale. Some claimants received roof replacement costs on roofs that they were planning to replace anyway. Most insurance companies gave a flat fee of $200 for food spoiled in refrigerators or thrown out because of the loss of electricity. Many people collected the money, whether or not they actually lost much food.[54]

Most people who cheated on their insurance justified their claim by rationalizing that they were finally collecting after having paid their premiums for so many years, and that insurance rates would almost certainly be increased after the storm. Whether or not insurance premiums would actually go up was not clear in the first few months. What was clear, however, was that the major insurance companies would decrease their market share in the Florida area.[55]

Roofers from Hell

With the huge infusion of insurance money after the storm, and the need for a wide range of services, a serious labor shortage became immediately apparent in the southern part of the county. The promise of plentiful work attracted many workers from around the country to Dade County. Finding temporary housing for this new influx of workers posed a real problem— particularly after so many homes and apartment buildings had been destroyed in the storm. In Key Largo, just south of Homestead and Florida City, campgrounds quickly filled with construction workers. Rowdy workers were responsible for a significant increase in the number of thefts and assaults committed in the south end of the county and the northern Keys. In December, for example, the Key Largo authorities investigated a hundred felony cases—triple the number of cases during the year before. A series of drug stings, which resulted in eighty-one arrests, involved only ten local suspects. The others were people from out of town, many of whom were construction workers. Throughout the community, the phrase "roofers from hell" became widespread.[56]

Dan Stokes, a roofer from Morristown, Tennessee, felt that roofers like him provided a critically important service for the community. In many respects, Stokes believes, roofers are "a breed apart," a fact that has to do with the grueling nature of their work. "They're a different-type person. . . . It's a hard job. How many people want to go on a roof that is twenty degrees hotter than what the temperature is just to start out with? You walk out from the ground to the top of the roof, you change fifteen to twenty degrees automatically. The asphalt you work with is five hundred degrees when it gets to the roof. So that's in your face all day long. Or you're around it all day long. They're wild, . . . probably the majority of them have broken the law and have no regard for rules, law, human rights, anything like that." Stokes also believes that there is a significant prejudice against roofers because of the dirty nature of their work and the fact that a lot of roofers were responsible for taking people's money and not completing the jobs they had contracted after the hurricane. Stokes recalls a woman he had spoken to the night before, who told him that a roofer

came in her subdivision, sold about twenty jobs, took the money from her, did about half the work, and left town. And I come into the neighborhood last night for the first time that they even allowed anybody in there. The lady was real open to me. She hated every roofer she'd ever seen until she saw me. But she still had a little resentment in the back of her voice, I could tell, towards the whole situation— that's understandable.

What I see as a first impression, when you are dirty and working and doing your job, you're looked down on. Whether it's the people in offices, whether it's the people in the apartments, the tenants. Those dirty roofers. They're dirty; they got tar on their face. They got dust all over them and everything else. But if they weren't doing that, they wouldn't have a roof overhead, because the tenants aren't going to get up and do it.[57]

Stokes first realized that Hurricane Andrew might hit somewhere along the eastern seaboard a couple of days before the storm. At that time, he had no idea that he might come to South Florida to help in the recovery process. The storm quickly affected him, however, in ways that he had not anticipated. In the area where he lived, around Morristown, Tennessee, for example, the prices for basic building supplies skyrocketed and materials soon became unavailable, he said. "At home . . . we had bid on several houses and the plywood, 2 x 4s, all the framing materials. The prices doubled. Then we weren't able to get them at all because it was all going to be coming here. . . . Whatever the hardware stores had at the time, we had to take our operating capital and buy as many quantities of anything we could buy to prevent a shortage. Also, the houses we were working on were bid houses, so anything extra that we spent on materials was coming out of our pockets."[58] Stokes had no intention of coming to Florida. His brother, who had been working in Alaska, stopped on his way south to rent some equipment from him. After working in South Florida for about two weeks, he called to see if Stokes would come down and help him on some jobs.

Before coming down, Stokes had a limited notion of how destructive the storm had been. "The media was real weak," as far as he was concerned, about giving people a sense of what the devastation was like from the storm. The reports he watched on television in Tennessee "really didn't even come close to mentioning what actually happened here as far as the devastation and damage and all that. Nothing, as far as personal damage. They'd show a little bit here and there, you know, because the people were homeless. I think maybe the first week there was real good coverage showing people trying to get back in their houses with no water and no sewage and all that. But after that, it kinda fizzled out and they started focusing on the National Guard, which really didn't give a good picture of what was going on."[59]

Roofing work was so widely available for Stokes after the storm that he decided to move his family permanently to Florida. Before he could do so, however, he wanted his four-year-old daughter to complete preschool, and he had to sell his house in Tennessee. Being without his family was particularly difficult for him. "I miss my family. I miss my kids. I guess the way I avoid dwelling on it maybe is to absorb myself in my work. So if I work fifteen to twenty hours a day . . ." Stokes typically worked seven days a week, taking a day off perhaps once every three weeks. The stress caused by his being away from home was significant. His daughter, for example, was having more difficulty in school than normal. As he explained, "In order to get attention I think, maybe she gets in trouble to create some attention." His absence also put a significant strain on his wife. "It's real hard on my wife, because she . . . raises two kids. She's a registered physical therapist. And she has a full-time job, plus raises the kids, plus whatever things need to be done around the house."[60]

The arrival of roofers from other parts of the country was an absolute necessity for the recovery to be able to get underway in South Florida. Many roofing companies, like other businesses in South Florida, found themselves unable to get their businesses going in the first few weeks after the storm. Nora Porobic, an independent roofing contractor, said, "We were out of business and had nowhere to operate out of for three weeks, and for two weeks were not even able to receive phone calls."[61] Workers, seeing opportunities with other companies, quit their jobs with Porobic.

In the weeks and months that followed the storm, roofing contractors found themselves frustrated by changing standards and codes. According to Stokes, regulations involving the use of tin roofing caps changed constantly. "The spacing of them has been different since day one. One day it was four inches on the laps, six inches staggered in the center, and eight inches on the end rolls. The next it's six inches on the laps, eight inches staggered, whatever." Both Stokes and Porobic were angry at the local building and inspection system. They complained about inconsistent regulations, as well as the fact that there had been such poor enforcement of codes in the area when the buildings were initially built and inspected. Stokes, for example, felt that "the insurance companies shouldn't be made to rebuild these houses, because of the stuff that went on in this county ten years ago. That should be the county or the city, not the insurance company. Period. They're getting ripped off. The codes weren't enforced. That's not the insurance companies' fault. That's the Dade County inspectors at fault. That's the City of Kendall's fault. That's the City of Miami's fault. . . . They soaked these insurance companies big time."[62]

Failed Building Codes

Before the storm, experts had anticipated that the main damage from a major hurricane such as Andrew would come from the storm surge. But Hurricane Andrew turned out to be a very dry storm. Damage inland was much greater than anticipated and was almost entirely wind related.[63] Damage to homes in the south part of Dade County did not necessarily correspond with where the highest winds from the storm were recorded. After analyzing sixty thousand damage inspection reports, the *Miami Herald* concluded that how recently a house had been built and the quality of its construction was crucial to whether or not it survived the storm. Houses built since 1980 were 68 percent more likely to be uninhabitable than were the homes that had been built earlier. A report after the storm compiled by an independent engineering company concluded that 70 percent of 121 homes inspected in areas with winds under 120 miles per hour had damage directly traceable to code violations and poor workmanship. Based on computer analyses conducted by the *Miami Herald*, it was determined that in the area between Kendall Drive and Southwest 184th Street, houses built after 1980 were likely to suffer three times as much damage as homes built before 1980.[64]

Among the most devastated housing developments in the county was Country Walk. Inspections after the storm indicated that roof braces were often sloppily attached, and that gable ends widely used throughout the complex were particularly vulnerable. The *Miami Herald*'s computer analysis showed that of the 90 percent of the homes in Country Walk that had been evaluated for insurance purposes (936 wood frame units), 98.2 percent were uninhabitable. In South Miami Heights Manor, a subdivision built in the early 1960s, 68 percent (765 concrete block units) of the homes were inspected for insurance purposes. Only 2.5 per cent of these structures were uninhabitable. Winds in the South Miami Heights Manor subdivision were recorded as being higher than those in the Country Walk area. Hurricane damage was, according to Peter Black, a scientist with the

National Oceanographic and Aeronautic Administration, "proportional to the kind of construction used." Single-story, older, concrete block buildings did better than newer, two-story, wood frame construction buildings.[65]

According to meteorologist Brian Norcross, a lot of houses would have been damaged but not totally destroyed by the storm if the intention of the building code had been upheld better throughout the county. The building code, he believes, "was not a prescriptive code. It was a code of intent, and for years that worked until people found out ways that fulfilled in some cases the letter of the coding and also not even that—but certainly not the intent of the code. The intent of the code was that the house had to be strong. And that was really the bottom line of the code."[66]

Norcross also strongly believes that storm shutters ought to be a required part of building any home in South Florida. "I have been saying for years it ought to be part of building a house. I think it's not just in the interest of the person that buys the house. I think it's in the community's interest not to have various areas of destruction in the community. It hurts things economically. You end up with this whole, huge mess." Norcross believes that it would be in the government's and the community's interest to have homes built with storm shutters as an integral part of their design. According to Norcross, it would not even necessarily mean more expensive houses, just slightly smaller ones. "It doesn't cost a dime more to build a house with shutters than it does one without shutters. It's just that the house might end up being 6 percent smaller. . . . It's not a matter of raising the price of the house, it is a matter of designing shutters into the house so that they fit into the overall pricing structure that you have determined."[67]

Relocating and Rebuilding

At the same time that she was supervising her own home repairs, Vida Pernick was trying to run her real estate business. In particular, she was trying to find rentals for clients who desperately needed a place to live. Pernick had spent the first four or five nights after the hurricane with her sister, who had electricity and air-conditioning. Each morning she left at

6:30 A.M. to drive back down south to her own home. But soon, the traffic became too difficult to make the trip. She was then able to stay with friends who had electricity and lived much closer to her own home.

Immediately after the hurricane, people in the real estate business were questioning the long-term impact of the storm. According to Pernick: "First of all, immediately, nobody could reach anybody. Phones were down and it was difficult to talk to people. Once we did meet with people, I guess the concern was, What's going to happen with real estate? And everybody was trying to use [Hurricane] Hugo as an example—that the market would be very strong, people would rebuild, and then, probably within two years, it would go back to normal."[68]

She quickly discovered, however, that housing had become the critical issue. Finding a rental for clients who were displaced was one of the most important things she had ever done. She worked at convincing established clients who weren't living in their condos during the summer to rent some of their property. One such client, who was in New York, was persuaded to rent his Kendall condominium to a couple whose home in Country Walk had been totally wiped out. "They moved into a two-bedroom apartment . . . it's a couple, a young married couple. She's pregnant. They moved in with her mother and father, whose house was also destroyed, and, I think, a sister. So they're living in a two-bedroom apartment. It worked out okay because the living room had a sleeper couch and the two bedrooms were available for both couples."[69] The main problem Pernick faced with placing people in rentals was that most people only wanted to rent a place for six months. This led to some price gouging on the part of owners, because people were so desperate to find a place to live.

Pernick was deluged with calls those first days after the hurricane. Everywhere she went, her portable phone was ringing. "It's a network here. I've been a real estate agent for fourteen or fifteen years and almost everybody who has been in the business for a while knows me. So when you get a rental, there's no time even to put it in the newspaper. Nor do we expect that we're going to try and protect our own interests in it by advertising it ourselves and renting it. . . . I would call the larger companies . . . and I told these various agents that I have an availability. . . . It was unbelievable, people looking for housing."[70]

Jeffrey Jenkins remembers the trouble Ernest ("Monkey") and his wife, Dee, had finding a place to live. "They had a hard time finding housing to accommodate a handicapped person. Right now, Monkey is living in a two-bedroom apartment with seven children, two grandchildren, and no handicap access. But it was all they could find."[71]

Many people made the decision to sell their homes and relocate. For some, it was a decision based on the need to get away from the depressing conditions of their neighborhood. There were some people, such as the Schorle family, who decided to leave South Florida altogether. Others knew they simply could not handle, emotionally and physically, the rebuilding process. Some did not have time to supervise contractors and workers rebuilding their homes. Once they got the insurance money for the damage to their home, many people paid off their mortgage and then sold the property at land value. Vida Pernick gave the example of someone who bought property for about $80,000 ten years ago. They got a mortgage at the time for $60,000, which was paid down to, say, $50,000. Their house was now insured for $160,000 because that's what it would cost to replace it. Pernick said that if they got $150,000 from their insurance company and paid off their mortgage, "they now have $100,000 in their pocket. They now turn around and sell the property for land value, which is—right after the hurricane—$18,000 to $25,000. . . . Now [November] it's gone up a little. Let's say they get $30,000. So now they have $130,000 cash in their pocket that they're going to move either up to North Dade or Broward or over to the West Coast . . . and buy a house that's worth $160,000 and either pay it all off in cash or get financing and put it into their pocket."[72] The decision of where to relocate was usually a difficult one. Of course, property had to be available in a particular area. Job locations and traffic patterns had to be considered, as well as schools. Often, there simply wasn't time to get to know a neighborhood, and people made mistakes. Families just wanted to get into a house and get on with their lives.

By the beginning of November, it was estimated that approximately 90,000 people would move as a result of Hurricane Andrew—more than half of them permanently out of Dade and Broward Counties. In South Dade, 61,000 adults, or approximately 42 percent of the adult population, were not living in their own homes. Many were living with friends or relatives elsewhere. Close to 11,000 of these people had rented a second residence.[73]

Among those who decided to relocate, many were retirees in the southern part of the county. Bill Blagriff, for example, had moved down from Schenectady, New York, three years before Andrew. In his mid-sixties, he had considered Homestead a Shangri-La before Hurricane Andrew and never dreamed of leaving the area. After the storm, however, he and his wife decided that rebuilding would be too difficult to justify staying, he said. "We'd love to stay in Homestead because we loved it here so much. But at our age, it looks like a tremendous rebuilding job. We haven't got that long left."[74]

In addition to the out-migration of retirees from South Dade as a result of the storm, many elderly citizens of the county had to move, because thirty-eight retirement homes and six nursing homes remained closed three months after the hurricane. How many friendships were disrupted as older adults were moved to new facilities in other parts of the county or state? What was it like for them to lose the familiar, the expected?[75]

Many young people found themselves out of work and needing to find opportunities elsewhere in the country. Others simply wanted to get out of Dade County and away from the depressing destruction, so they moved north to Broward County, which had suffered relatively little damage in the hurricane. Sales at Weston, an Arvida Corporation housing development in Broward, increased from 400 in 1991 to 825 in 1992. Most of the increase was attributed to victims of Hurricane Andrew relocating.[76]

Fundamental problems not only in the construction but also in the siting of buildings became a major issue after the storm. Approximately three thousand homeowners with damaged homes built below current federal flood-plain elevation standards found themselves required to raise their homes above flood level if the damage they incurred from the hurricane was more than 50 percent of the property's value. The cost of elevating most houses was about $30,000—none of which was covered by insurance. People in areas such as Saga Bay suddenly found themselves not only living in homes that had been seriously affected by the storm, but with large, additional costs beyond what their insurance was going to cover. It became impossible for many of them to consider rebuilding.[77]

Paul Shaffer found out in October that the 50/50 rule applied to his damaged home at 16105 Southwest Seventy-eighth Avenue. He had known about the complications with the 50/50 rule.

> They were having problems, so I knew about what was going on with regards to the 50/50 rule. I also knew about the dispute with the county, and the home owners, and Lennar, and for all I know, the Army Corps of Engineers, and the White House, and everybody else [who] was involved at that point. But it seemed relatively contained to that geographical neighborhood. It didn't seem like it applied to everybody. Then the *Miami Herald* came out with this little map of the flood zones, and where the surges were. . . . And we noticed we were right in line for the worst of the surge, the Deering Bay Estates. And yet, there were no floods.

Shaffer had already started working on his roof. But once the map from the *Herald* came out, Shaffer and his neighbors found out that they were affected by the 50/50 rule: "One of our neighbors got the heebie-jeebies . . . [so] he went to FEMA, saw the maps, and said, 'We're in trouble, folks.' So three of our neighbors went out, and they got independent surveyors to come in and do the surveying. Everybody's making a mad scramble to find their elevations. . . . Well, sure enough, everybody found out that they were within somewhere between 9 feet 3 inches at their doorstep, up to 10 feet." Shaffer's doorstep was at 9 feet 3 inches; according to FEMA, it had to be at 11 feet. All three of his neighbors were also under 11 feet. He had to call it quits on the roof repairs, "which, of course, left our roof in worse [shape] than it was before, because it had to be torn up and we didn't have it dried in. And of course it rained terribly right afterwards, so we had no dry-in at all. And no tarpaulin—no nothing."[78]

He already had a business trip to Washington, D.C., planned, so he decided to try to talk to people at FEMA. After repeatedly trying to get his phone calls to FEMA returned, Shaffer began to pull strings through family connections and finally got an appointment. An engineer, an administrator, an insurance specialist, and at least two other people were present at the meeting. After explaining the history of the legislation, the FEMA representatives made it clear that the law made it impossible for flood insurance money to be used to elevate a house. Whatever the cost, Shaffer had to pay to elevate his home or move out of the area. He left the meeting feeling that FEMA was in a weird position. "It was an agency created after the law which created the flood insurance program and other national relief programs. They were created to administer all these programs, so they had no say in what they were going to administer."[79]

It was going to cost Shaffer $75,000 to elevate his house and $180,000 to repair it—a total rebuilding package of $255,000. After lengthy negotiations with his insurance company, he was able to get a settlement of $213,000. Shaffer and his wife, Laurie, decided to tear down the existing house and build a new home at an elevation of twelve feet. Ironically, a week before we interviewed him for the Hurricane Andrew Oral History Research Project, Shaffer had found out that another article had come out that stated that the charts were indeed wrong, and that he could have gotten an exemption. He would have to pay higher flood insurance rates, but he wouldn't have to elevate his house. The Shaffers decided to "do it right" and tear down the old house and build a new one at twelve feet.

Shaffer's children went to school that year in Maryland, where they were living with Paul's parents while their home in Miami was being rebuilt. Despite all the bureaucratic aggravation and the logistical difficulties, he and his wife were having fun building the new house. "Our kids are healthy and happy. They are doing wonderfully in school. Laurie and I are healthy and happy. We've been having a fun time now. . . . The hurricane gave us the honeymoon we've never had—in a trailer out in front of a destroyed home. We had a three-month honeymoon."[80]

Repairing and rebuilding proved to be an enormously time-consuming and difficult process for most people. Supplies were difficult to obtain, contractors were often undependable, and prices were inflated. As Elizabeth Garcia Granados explained: "Everything has been more difficult than it should have been. For instance, to get a roofer to come out and repair the tile, to patch up the place where the tiles fell off, that's difficult. Getting people to replace the awning, the carport, it's impossible. Nobody will do it. So it's just taking much longer. Everything is . . . more pressure, more stressful."[81] Ernest Jenkins and his wife, Dee, had many problems trying to rebuild their home. It took months to get the tile that made it easier for him to operate his wheelchair. Then they had to get the ramps for the wheelchair rebuilt.[82] Most people in South Dade who were involved in rebuilding their homes learned to wait—in lines at the stores, for contractors and workers, for insurance adjusters and inspectors, and even for checks to clear the bank.

Damien Kong was afraid that it might take longer to rebuild Metrozoo than it took to build it in the first place. "It wasn't like when the zoo was being built. So that is another problem. Contractors and things that normally wouldn't charge us an arm and a leg now have access to so much that they don't have to take [our job] or want to work for us. They can work for a lot of other people. So we're having a hard time getting contractors to do a lot of the work." Replacement trees were a major issue for the zoo. "There are no trees out there on the market for us, and on top of that, the asking price for these trees is astronomical. So right now nobody's replacing trees. If we can, we'll look for trees outside in other areas; . . . we're looking for a reasonable price, . . .we can't start out with little four-inch-pot trees. We have to get mature trees; . . .we need to get the animals shaded. This morning I went out to the chimp exhibit, and they had these little clusters of coral rock, and there were three of them sitting in the middle, hiding from the sun because the sun was just blazing down on top of them."[83]

Allen Farrington, a contractor, found that all the people he was working with before the hurricane wanted to get their houses back into shape so they could live in them. "In my experience, the people in the abandonment process are the ones who have very little capital in the house. The people that have a lot of capital in the house just wanted to get them fixed and get back into them—with the exception of the people who live in the Saga Bay area."[84]

Lennox and Alicia Jeffers decided to rebuild and remodel their home. "This makes me feel better," said Alicia, "to know we're remodeling. You know, some people just want their house the way it was. But we decided to go ahead and remodel."[85] The Jefferses had commuted daily for two weeks from a friend's house, immediately after the hurricane. They lived in their house for a little while and then moved into a trailer, so the rebuilding and remodeling could begin. Lennox Jeffers found living in the trailer for two months another difficult situation. "From living in a home to moving into a trailer was a big change, because it was very confined . . . for me, it was somewhat difficult living in such a closed space. Since we have moved back into the house, to part of the house (we have two bedrooms that are now functional), . . . it still remains a major problem, in the sense that we don't have places to invite guests in. . . . But, day-to-day, there seems to be an improvement."[86] Lennox expected it to take about four years for everyone's house in his neighborhood to be restored and the trees and landscaping to be replaced.

Making sure that houses in South Florida would be better able to weather future hurricanes was an issue that concerned many people in South Florida after Andrew. Perhaps no single group demonstrated this concern as much as Habitat for Humanity.

Habitat for Humanity

After the storm, Habitat for Humanity, which had already been active in building projects in South Dade, undertook the reconstruction of most of a city block in Homestead. Volunteers, including approximately fifty students from West Virginia University who had come to South Florida specifically to help in the reconstruction process, rebuilt the thousand-square-foot homes.[87]

Habitat for Humanity's long-term plans for Dade County included the construction of two hundred homes over a two-year period in the area struck by Hurricane Andrew. Between October 1992 and February 1993, six three-bedroom homes were completed in South Dade. Applicants for Habitat homes, in both Dade and other parts of the country, are required to hold regular jobs and to contribute four hundred hours of volunteer work.[88]

Betty Holmes, a Head Start teacher's assistant who lived in the south part of the county, was one of the people to qualify for a Habitat for Humanity Home. Holmes's apartment had been totally destroyed by the hurricane. As she explained: "My kids' rooms, they [the walls] caved in. And in my bedroom, the wall was split in half. It's a two-story house. The clothes, the furniture—it was all a mess."[89]

Holmes had not stayed in her home during the storm but had gone to her mother's house. She was convinced that she and her four children would have been killed if they had remained in her apartment. "We went back the day after and I cried . . . I have no insurance—renters' insurance

. . . I didn't know anything about it . . . everything was ruined."[90] After the hurricane, Holmes and her three children and adopted nephew stayed at her mother's house. They were five of the total of twelve family members her mother took in after Andrew, despite the fact that she herself had lost two bedrooms, a bath, and every window in her house.

Holmes considered a Habitat house her "saving grace." She applied with her sister. She explained that she knew that

you had to have a job to get it, you couldn't be unemployed. They prefer working people with a family. I don't know how they did the salary. They called her first, not me, and I was thinking that maybe they checked my credit, and I thought that was a problem for me. So then the Habitat man said my file was not complete. I needed to take my W2 and a check stub and give it to them for verification. Then the next week they told my sister to meet them again, but not me. I went along anyway, and I asked about my application, and a week later they called me at work. But I was at a workshop at Metro-Dade so I didn't get the message on Friday.

When I came to work Monday I got the message they'd called. So I kept calling Monday, Tuesday, and the lady wasn't in. . . . She was out in the field. Finally, she called me on Thursday . . . and told me, and I was saying "Hooray! For real? For real? Oh, my God!" I told all my co-workers, and I thought, "This is my blessing."[91]

After finding out that she had been chosen to participate in the program, Holmes was told to meet on the building site on the following Saturday at 7:30 in the morning. Children under sixteen were not allowed on the site.

From the beginning, it was made clear to Holmes that she would have to contribute significantly to the building of her own house. "You have to put in a lot of sweat. Four hundred hours, altogether, before you can get the deed to the house. . . . All six houses have to be built before you can move in. So everybody has to help everybody. If one is finished, and the next one isn't, you have to help them. It's not like you're just worried about yourself . . . you work on everybody's house. It's a Christian organization and people." Holmes had never had any experience building, but she was given training on the spot. "I even helped put up the frame . . . there's a lot of lifting and when one side of the frame was up, we applauded! It's fun, you get a lot of experience. A lot of men never did this before either. But a lot of people supervise . . . they want to have all six houses ready for December. But before we can move in, the family has to do one hundred hours themselves. Each person gets credit, no matter how long or short [a time] they work."[92]

Habitat for Humanity was not the only group concerned with rebuilding homes that were lost as a result of Hurricane Andrew. Six months after the storm, the group We Will Rebuild approved funding for three groups to construct or repair 219 homes in South Dade. A total of $1.025 million in grants was awarded by the group to construct forty-one new single-family homes in Goulds and seventy-eight new rental units in Richmond Heights, and to repair a hundred homes throughout South Dade for residents who could not find other financial help.[93]

Homestead Air Force Base

Homestead Air Force Base was virtually wiped out by Hurricane Andrew. Damage was so widespread that the base's three fighter squadrons had to be moved to South Carolina and Georgia. The 309th Squadron, which had twenty-four F-16s, was sent to Shaw Air Force Base near Sumter, South Carolina. The 307th and 308th Squadrons, each with eighteen F-16s, were reassigned to Moody Air Force Base near Valdosta, Georgia.[94]

During the 1992 presidential campaign, President George Bush promised that Homestead Air Force Base would be rebuilt. Shortly after the hurricane, Congress approved the allocation of $76 million in reconstruction funds for the base. Total reconstruction costs for the base were estimated at approximately $500 million.

On March 12, 1993, Defense Secretary Les Aspin announced the closing of 31 major military bases and the reduction of operations at an additional 134 installations. Homestead Air Force Base was included among the major bases to be shut down. The base was the main economic anchor for the Homestead area. Employing 8,700 people, including 4,700 active military personnel, the air base generated an annual payroll of $152 million. About 21,000 military retirees lived in the vicinity of the base in order to be able to take advantage of commissary privileges. Military retirees collected an estimated $327 million in payroll. The total economic loss as a result of the closing of the base was estimated at $430 million per year.[95]

Human Losses

Estimating physical losses, such as the closing of Homestead Air Force Base, is much easier than determining the human loss. Although two weeks after the storm, the Dade County medical examiner had set the official death toll at thirty-five, storm-related deaths continued through the fall and into early winter. A *Miami Herald* report concluded that by the end of January 1993, at least eighty-five people had died of causes related to the storm. Of the twelve who died in automobile accidents after the storm, eight were killed as a result of accidents caused by downed or malfunctioning traffic lights. Five people committed suicide. Francisco Mercado, for example, who was upset over the destruction caused by Hurricane Andrew, shot himself in the chest a little more than two weeks after the storm. Jeffrey Gardner, a Southwestern Bell lineman from out of town, was electrocuted two months after the storm while installing an aerial cable. Candida Camporino fell three stories to her death three weeks after the storm from a balcony damaged by the hurricane.

At the same time, the emotional and psychological pressure people dealt with as a result of the storm began to emerge. By late December, the countywide divorce rate had jumped by nearly 30 percent; the number of parents giving up custody of their children had increased by 20 percent, countywide. A survey of 1,408 homes conducted by the *Miami Herald* indicated that 30 percent of the people in South Dade County were living with someone who was stressed to the point of losing control. More than 40 percent of the people surveyed indicated that they were living with someone who was having trouble sleeping, who was anxious, or who had thoughts of suicide.[96]

In October, two months after the storm, a survey of eighty-two children at Redondo Elementary School in Homestead conducted by John Shaw, director of Child and Adolescent Psychiatry at the University of Miami, showed that 83 percent were afraid or upset when they thought about the hurricane. When asked if the hurricane interfered with their homework,

69 percent said yes; 64 percent indicated that it was more difficult for them to pay attention in class. Sixty-seven percent of the children also indicated that they were more jumpy and nervous than before Hurricane Andrew and were having nightmares.[97]

The Homestead High School Marching Band

Perhaps one of the most dramatic events in the months following Hurricane Andrew was the appearance of the Homestead High School Marching Band at the presidential inauguration of William Jefferson Clinton on January 20, 1993. As the sixty students marching in the band went by the presidential reviewing stand in front of the White House, Bill Clinton stood and applauded them. It was an emotional moment for Sherrod Gilley. "When I saw President Clinton, the smile on his face, just him knowing that we were coming here, it made me feel good. When I saw Clinton, my heart really went into it. When he jumped up, it just made me play even better."[98]

The trip to Washington by bus had taken twenty-one hours. It was the first time that many of the students had been out of Florida.[99] Most of them had been profoundly affected by the storm. Much of their free time during the fall had been spent helping repair their homes in Homestead. Once they went back to school, they were very emotional, wondering which of their friends they were going to see. Who had been hurt by the storm? Or died? Or moved out of town (primarily because Homestead Air Force Base had closed)? Of the original 130 band members, only 55 had returned to school after the storm.

According to Rodester Brandon, the director of the Homestead band program, Hurricane Andrew had a tremendous impact on his band. "It was rough on them, because music requires you to give of yourself, from your inner sanctum. . . . I remember the first day of rehearsal, and the band was just kind of marching around and everything. It wasn't my band. My group is a lot more musical—a lot more involved." Brandon had to call his students together and explain to them that they were the same people they had been before the hurricane. They needed to play as they used to— even if their group was much smaller. He got up on his soapbox and tried to sound like the football coach. "Those guys, it was straight emotional.

You could sense the people crying, and people were really opening up from their inner self. When they got back on that field, man, it was like really nice. It was like, ah, there it is again. Yeah."[100]

After the hurricane, Brandon had been concerned that his profession, music, would not be of much interest to people who were busy dealing with the basic levels of existence. As he was living through the process of rebuilding his own home, he was worried about whether or not he could be effective in his work at the high school. He really did not want to do the band program that fall. But then he heard about the football team out there practicing on the field. "I was thinking, 'How the heck were they going to practice when they got their houses messed up?' But you know, that time of the year is real big for them. It depends a whole lot upon the rest of the guys who are getting ready for scholarships and stuff like that. So they really couldn't let the football program go, and a lot of that was to do with the coach, I think. He was just really pushing it. You know, moving things along." Once he got the kids in the band "fired up," the band program got going as though the hurricane had never come. The only problem, according to Brandon, was an emotional one: The kids were not able to "give" of themselves as they had before. They were sheltering themselves. Brandon felt that marching in the inaugural parade "did a lot for the emotions of the students. . . . I think that this was the only thing that made it possible for us to not lose this group emotionally. I noticed for the first time, people were really smiling from their hearts and their souls, rather than just these outward smiles."[101]

When asked if he felt there were any positive outcomes as a result of Hurricane Andrew, Brandon mentioned people helping each other. In his personal life, "Andrew was a blessing, it really was. . . . Personally, I have a brand new house. The same house, but, boy, that house is better than any kind of a house I would imagine living in. Because of my settlement, I was able to pay off all of my debts." Brandon also appreciated the fact that he now knew a lot of his neighbors that he didn't know that well before the hurricane. "We eat together, we share together. We're talking to each other—we hadn't done that before." He felt that he had been able to use his music as a way of causing nice things to happen in a way that would not have been possible before the hurricane. "Hurricane Andrew was an act of God. Generally, when we talk about acts of God, we are talking about tragedy. . . . But I think if Hurricane Andrew was an act of God, this is God trying, making his effort to emphasize to us how important it is to share, and to help out, to help each other and work together."[102]

Not all of the voices in this book would agree with Rodester Brandon's feeling that Hurricane Andrew was a blessing. Most, however, would agree that if any good came out of Andrew, it probably had to do with people getting to know each other and helping other people—not just neighbors, but strangers, as well.

Life Will Never Be the Same

7

There are natural disasters that define a community and remain forever prominent in its memory. The 1889 flood in Johnstown, Pennsylvania, is such an event, as is the 1900 Galveston, Texas, flood. In 1969, Hurricane Camille left its mark indelibly along the Mississippi coast.

In South Florida, the 1926 category 4 hurricane that struck Miami Beach and Miami represents a turning point in the region's history. The storm brought an abrupt end to the land boom. As a result, the Depression

Typical of the humorous signs that were common despite the storm's devastation. (Image ID: wea00564)

came to South Florida three years earlier than to the rest of the country. The storm served as an economic, social, and ecological marker.

In much the same way, Hurricane Andrew was a crucial benchmark for South Florida during the last decade of the twentieth century. In the nearly ten years since Hurricane Andrew struck, almost everything in South Florida's history—and particularly the southern half of Dade County—has come to be referred to in terms of pre– or post–Hurricane Andrew.

Many of the losses the community felt as a result of the hurricane simply could not be replaced. As Mary Oldiges, director of the Parent Resource Center, explained: "There's such an overwhelming sense of loss. Not just material things, but things that were familiar. A favorite tree, a street you turned down on the way home. For a child, . . . a mother and father now treating you differently."[1] Diane Allen, who was born and raised in Homestead, but now lives in Utah, came back to visit the family home at Thanksgiving. For her, the familiar and the comfortable setting she had always known were gone. As she explained: "Our house is in a wooded area—or it was, shall I say. The immediate neighborhood and the main streets look so different. We used to live between an old hammock and a pine forest. So many of those trees are gone. Home is not at all what it used to be."[2] Deana Granger, who returned for Thanksgiving to South Dade from Connecticut after having been gone a year, said: "It's sad. You just don't recognize the place where you grew up."[3]

And yet, there was a renewal going on. Martin J. Carney noticed it. On September 14, when the university opened for the fall term, he had walked across campus and become very concerned that the landscaping would never be beautiful again. He didn't think it could happen. Three months later when he was interviewed, he was amazed "to see how nature has begun to [renew] . . . things are growing back already, and blooms are on the trees, and things like that. To see that, it has been a powerful metamorphosis, so to speak. It has been kind of touching. We couldn't have expected that—for nature to take its course. We have all read that, I guess, even as a kid in biology. But to see that actually happen, it has been pretty moving."[4]

Susan Schorle believed the hurricane brought out the best and worst in people. It made her realize how "fragile" life is. The experience of the storm also made her reconsider her priorities. Increasingly, she found herself asking, "Exactly what's important and what isn't?"[5]

Others also noticed that people felt more vulnerable after Hurricane Andrew. Howard Camner, a writer and poet, explained that the storm made him "a lot more sensitive" to how fragile people are. It also changed how he approached his day-to-day life. "I live from day to day. I've always wanted to live in the now. Well, now I live in the now."[6]

Some people talked about how their outlook on the world was changed by the experience of Hurricane Andrew. Pat Warren explained how the storm was beyond anything she had anticipated.

> It changed me completely. I'm not the same person. There has been a pre-Andrew, and now there is a post-Andrew. . . . I just wasn't anticipating anything like what happened—in no way. And I learned one thing—you are on your own. If anything major happens like what happened, you have to go and get ice for yourself. You have to go for the generator. To me, it was frightening because, for some reason, I thought somebody was going to come in or somebody would be here. I don't know who, but like FPL, or whatever, they would be there. Nobody was there. It is only the basic family unit. It is what you depend on. Your neighbors and friends are taking care of their needs. I never expected anything like that.[7]

LaWanda Scott, a day care worker at the Canterbury Preschool, University of Miami, said that the hurricane continued to haunt her months after the storm. "I say it hasn't affected me, when in actuality it has devastated me and I can't deal with it. I keep trying to escape, trying to run away. But I can't. It's everywhere. I am seeing a counselor because I can't sleep. I'm not eating properly and I am emotionally drained. . . . When I hear the wind or the rain begins to fall, I think the hurricane might be coming back." Scott perceived her colleagues at the preschool as "trying to suppress everything. But the scary part is that all of this will resurface when we least expect it. No one is honestly dealing with their feelings. Everyone is trying to hide. But we can only wear a mask for so long. Our true faces will soon be revealed."[8]

Art Carlson had similar feelings.

There isn't a day that goes by that I don't think about the storm. Our family was very, very lucky. I mean, we were essentially untouched by the storm. But, there isn't a day that goes by that we don't think about it, that we don't see the physical reminders around us here in the neighborhood, that we don't think that it's, like, only two months until the next hurricane season rolls around. Every time I walk by all these windows, you know, it's like, I know we've got shutters, but we ought to have more. I mean, this house that we're in now was built in 1905, and it's weathered the worst. And it came through Andrew without a problem at all, as close as we are to the bay. But nevertheless, there's always that concern. It's always in the back of my mind. And it's probably never going to go away.[9]

Hurricane Andrew also profoundly affected Paul Dee and how he came to look at life and things in general. "I look at things totally different now. Personal property—cars and objects and my home—are all replaceable. My view is increasingly that the most important thing is my relationship with other people. What became really important for me was the emotional structure of my family and my friends. In my office, a quarter of the people I worked with lost their homes. I think more now about how what I do is going to affect other human beings. That's all that really matters. The other stuff is really irrelevant."[10]

Even among people who stayed on in South Florida, the idea of leaving the area was increasingly appealing in the month following the storm. Art Carlson and his wife, for the first time in their lives, talked seriously about leaving the area, Carlson said.

I'm a Grove native. I mean, I love the Grove. I've never really wanted to live anywhere else. I took seven years out living in Kendall, which was the god-awfulest, biggest mistake I ever made in my life. But I've always loved the Grove. My wife loves the Grove. She's lived here for many years. But since the storm, we have been seriously talking. We talked before, but now [we are] seriously talking about moving to places like Montana or Wyoming. And I would say that that's essentially because of the storm, and the possibility of having to go through all this again. It's just flat-out frightening, and we haven't completely gotten ourselves settled since then.[11]

In fact, Carlson did eventually leave the area, relocating with his family to Montana.

The consequences of Hurricane Andrew will take years to assess. There is little doubt that for the majority of the people in the southern half of the county, the storm will remain a major moment or event in their lives. For the larger Miami community, Hurricane Andrew may represent a significant shared experience that creates important bonds between people. Malcom Kahn, a counselor at the University of Miami, explained that the storm might have caused people to stick together more, "in a greater common share of interests. . . . Miami, in a way, has improved its self-esteem by the way it coped with the storm."[12] For James White the storm created a greater awareness, a greater humanism in the community. "People have come together. . . . There is a humanism that has come over South Dade and Dade County, as well as outside of Dade County, that I've never seen in my life. It's beautiful to see people helping people."[13]

Officer Jane Jones felt that for a short period of time, at least, everybody was working together—citizens, law enforcement, and the military. "Everybody was a team," she said, "and that was positive. You'd see a Cuban guy, a black guy, a Jewish guy—all working together, trying to get to the same goal."[14] Michael Tang was really proud to be a police officer, "kind of like the old days when the primary responsibility was to help people. It wasn't about chasing bad guys; . . . they [the police] were helpers, servants of the community."[15]

At the Seaquarium, Richard Howard considered the hurricane a plus, from a personnel standpoint. "There are a lot of people around here now who are highly respected—not to suggest that they weren't respected before. They were just here, doing their job, and nobody paid much attention. We now know that so-and-so, who works over there, was a real hero during the storm and after the storm and got in and helped clean out dead sharks when nobody wanted to get in there and do it."[16]

University of Miami president Edward T. Foote II considered the rebuilding process after the storm to be an important moment in the formation of the Miami community and the university. "I think we are going to be a better, not a worse, institution because of the storm. Thank God we escaped catastrophic damage. We were damaged, but not irreparably damaged. On the plus side, we went through an experience that made us better people."[17]

« »

Throughout the interviews conducted for this book, we hardly ever heard the storm referred to as an "act of God." One exception was Rodester Brandon. He considered the hurricane a blessing and believed that it was God's way of trying to make us realize how important it is to help each other and to work together.[18] Pat Ashley had a slightly different point of view.

> I have no sense that God is pulling puppet strings so that we learn our lesson, but I am grateful for the lessons . . . to come out of it and for the experience that it has been. The whole recognition of God's presence in the storm, out of the storm, after the storm, sustaining people, suffering with people—not distant, not directing things, but moving as part of it. Part of it is sort of facing the toughness of how, although I don't see God as a puppet master, I have to acknowledge God's responsibility in that God did not keep it from happening. So there's a sense of saying what a radical respect God has for the freedom of all creation, not to intervene. Part of it is leading us to recognize our own responsibility. We live in a place where hurricanes happen. None of us can claim ignorance about knowing that. We were just sort of innocent about what it really meant.[19]

Now that we know what it means to prepare for, live through, and rebuild after a major hurricane, we, the authors, know that we will never, ever again try to assure ourselves or someone else by saying, "Oh, I'm sure it's going to be all right." We now understand that we are all vulnerable. As Ana Veciana-Suarez, a columnist for the *Miami Herald,* wrote one year after the storm: "As are so many things in life, this inescapable lesson in vulnerability was painful. It has made me realize that nobody is exempt from the forces of nature, that everybody has to pay dues somehow, sometime."[20] We understand that whatever we have can be taken away from us. Questions such as Why me? and What have I done to deserve this? really have no answer. We do know, however, that even in an age when we can travel in space and unlock genetic codes, we still cannot stop a hurricane or an earthquake.

Life will never be the same after an experience like Hurricane Andrew. Through our interviewees, we have come to better understand the storm and the consequences of such a natural disaster for the community. The experience of Hurricane Andrew forced South Floridians to address their own vulnerability and the fragility of the environment, to accept the inevitability of natural disasters and their impact on their lives. It also gave them the chance to demonstrate the strength of human beings to rebuild and go on in the most challenging circumstances possible.

But as the storm fades in memory, the South Florida community needs to remember its lessons. In 1994, at the time of the second anniversary of Hurricane Andrew, Ana Veciana-Suarez recalled the type of silent promise people made during that period when their patience and fortitude were being tested: "Not to work late so often. To pay more attention to our children. Not to worry about buying the latest of anything. To visit old relatives more often. To laugh loudly, and to dance whenever possible. To forgive more honestly. To learn something we've never gotten around to learning. To treat ourselves more gently."[21]

Have South Floridians forgotten the lessons of Andrew? *Weren't they supposed to last a lifetime?* Aren't they lessons relevant to all Americans? By listening to the voices of the people in this book, who lived through what is widely acknowledged as the worst natural disaster in American history and moved on to rebuild their lives and our community, we hope that all of us will be reminded of lessons that we should never forget.

Notes

Chapter 1. "It's Going to Be Very, Very Bad"

1. "Andrew, Recovery by Numbers," *Miami Herald*, August 24, 1994; *Fort Lauderdale Sun-Sentinel* staff, *Andrew!* 5.

2. Curtis Morgan and Stephen K. Doig, "Could It Happen Again?" *Miami Herald*, September 5, 1992.

3. Hurricanes were not given names until 1950.

4. Interview with Bob Sheets conducted by Lauren Markoff and Eugene F. Provenzo, Jr., March 3, 1993, National Hurricane Center, Miami.

5. Parks, "Until Last Week, Storm of '26 Was *the* Hurricane," *Miami Herald*, August 30, 1992.

6. *Fort Lauderdale Sun-Sentinel* staff, *Andrew!* 15.

7. John Donnelly, "Expert: Savage Whirlwind Intensified Andrew's Fury," *Miami Herald*, January 20, 1993. These vortices probably lasted for ten seconds and spun at 80 miles per hour. When combined with the 120–mile-per-hour movement of the storm, this gave them the 200–mile-per-hour speed.

The Cutler Ridge Holiday Inn, north of Homestead, extensively damaged by Hurricane Andrew's winds. (Image ID: weao0550)

8. *Fort Lauderdale Sun-Sentinel* staff, *Andrew!* 8.

9. Interview with Vida Pernick conducted by Alisa Moeller, December 1, 1992, Miami (henceforth Pernick interview).

10. Interview with Alexis Martinez conducted by Beatriz Quintairos, November 8, 1992, Miami (henceforth Martinez interview).

11. Interview with Alicia Jeffers conducted by Allen C. Paul, April 17, 1993, Miami (henceforth A. Jeffers interview).

12. Interview with James White conducted by Pamela Abbey, November 2, 1992, Miami (henceforth White interview).

13. Interview with James Mooney conducted by Pamela E. Abbey, November 19, 1992, Miami (henceforth Mooney interview).

14. Interview with Eve McNanamy conducted by Ginger Williams, November 19, 1992, Miami (henceforth McNanamy interview).

15. A. Jeffers interview.

16. Interview with Lawrence Moose conducted by Karen G. Befeler-Neuhaus, November 20, 1992, Miami (henceforth Moose interview).

17. Interview with Florence T. Goldstein conducted by Denise Goldstein, March 17, 1993, Miami (henceforth Goldstein interview).

18. Interview with Edward T. Foote II conducted by Rebecca Hoffman, November 16, 1992, Miami (henceforth Foote interview).

19. Interview with Irene Baljet conducted by Billie Houston, November 6, 1992, Miami (henceforth Baljet interview).

20. Interview with Margaret Sowell conducted by Ginger Williams, November 18, 1992, Miami (henceforth Sowell interview).

21. Interview with Ronald V. Ponton conducted by Juliet E. Hart, November 25, 1992, Miami (henceforth Ponton interview).

22. Interview with Solomon Graham conducted by Dan Dalke, November 12, 1992, Miami (henceforth Graham interview).

23. Interview with Paul Douglas Shaffer conducted by Sally A. Shay, March 30, 1993, Miami (henceforth Shaffer interview).

24. Interview with Rodester Brandon conducted by Jill Goldston, 1993, Miami (henceforth Brandon interview).

25. Interview with Mike Puller conducted by Joan Dudas, December 7, 1992, Miami (henceforth Puller interview).

26. Interview with Mike Brescher conducted by Deborah Strand, April 12, 1993, Key Biscayne (henceforth Brescher interview).

27. Interview with Damien Kong conducted by Leslie Monreal, November 16, 1992, Miami (henceforth Kong interview).

28. Shaffer interview.

29. A. Jeffers interview.

30. Interview with John O. Cleveland conducted by Lyn Culbertson, March 6, 1993, Miami.

31. Interview with Pat Warren conducted by Mykel Mangrum, November 12, 1992, Miami (henceforth Warren interview).

32. Interview with Martin J. Carney conducted by Dan Dalke, October 17, 1992, Miami (henceforth Carney interview).

33. Interview with Eve A. Koenig conducted by Erika Sardi, December 2, 1992, Miami (henceforth Koenig interview).

34. Interview with Elizabeth Garcia Granados conducted by Bruce Bentley, October 28, 1992, Miami (henceforth Granados interview).

35. Interview with Howard Camner conducted by Raquel Fundora, November 26, 1992, Miami (henceforth Camner interview).

36. Interview with Richard W. Anderson conducted by Mykel Mangrum, November 25, 1992, Miami (henceforth Anderson interview).

Chapter 2. August 24, 1992

1. Norcross, "Hurricane Andrew."

2. John Dorschner, "The Hurricane That Changed Everything," *Miami Herald,* August 30, 1992.

3. Interview with Andrew Feldman conducted by Jennifer Caunedo, December 1992, Miami (henceforth Feldman interview).

4. Interview with Lisa Jacobson conducted by Jennifer Caunedo, December 1992, Miami (henceforth Jacobson interview).

5. Interview with Sergeant Michael Laughlin conducted by Lesley Sevastopulos, December 4, 1992, Miami (henceforth Laughlin interview).

6. Koenig interview.

7. Interview with Grace Laskis conducted by Lynne Katz, October 17, 1992, Miami (henceforth Laskis interview).

8. Interview with Karen Baldwin, conducted by Eugene F. Provenzo Jr., September 1, 1992, Miami (henceforth Baldwin interview).

9. This conversation appears on videocassette; see Norcross, "Hurricane Andrew."

10. Baldwin interview.

11. Interview with Faye McCloud, conducted by Sandra Fradd and Eugene F. Provenzo Jr., February 26, 1993, Miami (henceforth McCloud interview).

12. Ibid.

13. Sowell interview.

14. Ibid.

15. Ibid.

16. Foote interview.

17. Interview with Michael Tang conducted by Dan Jenkins, October 23, 1992, Miami (henceforth Tang interview).

18. Moose interview.

19. Interview with Cristina Quintairos conducted by Beatriz Quintairos, November 12, 1992, via telephone from Miami to Arlington, Va. (henceforth Quintairos interview).

20. Baljet interview.

21. Martinez interview.

22. Interview with Sharon Johnson conducted by Eugene F. Provenzo Jr. and Asterie Baker Provenzo, June 2, 1993, Miami (henceforth Johnson interview).

23. Interview with Art Carlson conducted by Lyn Culbertson, March 18, 1993, Miami (henceforth Carlson interview).

24. Interview with Ross McGill Jr. conducted by Marva Donaldson, October 30, 1992, Miami (henceforth McGill interview).

25. White interview.

26. Interview with Pat Ashley conducted by Billie Houston, October 27, 1992, Miami (henceforth Ashley interview).

27. Joan Fleischman, "Man-of-the-hour Norcross Gets Flood of Thanks, Proposals," *Miami Herald*, August 31, 1992.

28. Interview with Bryan Norcross conducted by Anna Rego and Eugene F. Provenzo Jr., April 6, 1993, Miami (henceforth Norcross interview).

29. Ibid.

30. Johnson interview.

Chapter 3. Coming Out after the Storm

1. Laughlin interview.

2. Johnson interview.

3. McCloud interview.

4. McGill interview.

5. White interview.

6. Laskis interview.

7. Baldwin interview.

8. Interview with Peter Schulz conducted by Deborah Strand, April 4, 1993, Miami (henceforth Schulz interview).

9. Puller interview.

10. Carlson interview.

11. Interview with Dan Piet conducted by Karen Heil, November 4, 1992, Ft. Lauderdale.

12. Interview with I. J. Hudson conducted by Eugene F. Provenzo Jr., August 27, 1992, Miami (henceforth Hudson interview).

13. Carlson interview.

14. Sowell interview.

15. Brescher interview.

16. Moose interview.

17. Laskis interview.

18. Warren interview.

19. Interview with Paul Dee conducted via telephone by Eugene F. Provenzo Jr., May 25, 1993, Miami (henceforth Dee interview).

20. Interview with Roberta Smith conducted by Tresca Whitehead-Jenkins, April 18, 1993, Coconut Grove, Fla. (henceforth R. Smith interview).

21. Baljet interview.

22. Ibid.

23. Ibid.

24. Ibid.

25. A. Jeffers interview.

26. Ibid.

27. Interview with Lennox Jeffers conducted by Paul C. Allen, April 17, 1993, Miami (henceforth L. Jeffers interview).

28. A. Jeffers interview.

29. Shaffer interview.

30. Ibid.

Chapter 4. Immediate Emergency Relief

1. Hudson interview.

2. Scott Higham, "Firefighters Fought More Than Blazes," *Miami Herald,* September 21, 1992.

3. Interview with Jane Jones (pseudonym used by female Metropolitan Dade County Police Officer) conducted by Dan Jenkins, January 8, 1993, Miami (henceforth Jones interview).

4. Tang interview.

5. Ibid.

6. Jones interview.

7. Tang interview.

8. Jones interview.

9. Laughlin interview.

10. Donna Gehrke, "In Perrine, Fear and Vigilance," *Miami Herald,* August 29, 1992.

11. Tang interview.

12. "Curfew Ends: Metro to Add Patrols, Resume 'Safe T' Program," *Miami Herald,* November 16, 1992.

13. Lisa Getter and Grace Lim, "Looters Add Insult to Andrew's Injury," *Miami Herald,* August 26, 1992.

14. Jones interview.

15. A. Jeffers interview.

16. Koenig interview.

17. Interview with Frank J. Da Silva Jr. conducted by Denise Goldstein, April 22, 1993, Miami (henceforth Da Silva interview).

18. Ibid.

19. Ibid.

20. Ibid.

21. Paul Anderson, Grace Lim, and Martin Merzer, "Chiles Seeks $9 Billion in Aid," *Miami Herald,* September 9, 1992.

22. Koenig interview; A. Jeffers interview.

23. Buddy Nevins, "The Second Disaster," in *Fort Lauderdale Sun-Sentinel* staff, *Andrew!* 28.

24. Lyskowski and Rice, *The Big One,* 16.

25. Kate Hale, August 27, 1992, quoted in Kleinberg, *The Florida Hurricane and Disaster,* 40.

26. Jessica Lee, "Support Is for the 'Long Haul,'" *USA Today,* September 1, 1992, 1.

27. Dexter Filkins, "Army General Faces Huge Relief Task," *Miami Herald,* August 30, 1992.

28. Jonathon King, "To the Rescue," in *Fort Lauderdale Sun-Sentinel* staff, *Andrew!* 52.

29. Laurence Jolidon, "Military's Peaceful Presence," *USA Today,* September 1, 1992, 2A.

30. Patrick May, "Here's the Bread-and-Butter Boat," *Miami Herald,* September 3, 1993.

31. Anderson, Lim, and Merzer, "Chiles Seeks $9 Billion."

32. King, "To the Rescue," 54.

33. Ibid.

34. Da Silva interview.

35. Ibid.

36. Pamela Ferdinand, "Makeshift Hospitals Tending to Wounded," *Miami Herald,* August 27, 1992.

37. Interview with Armando Santelices conducted by Eugene F. Provenzo, Jr., September 1, 1992, Homestead, Fla.

38. Interview with Bill Blackburn conducted by Eugene F. Provenzo Jr., September 1, 1992, Homestead, Fla.

39. Scott Higham, "The FEMA Disaster," *Miami Herald,* January 24, 1993.

40. Ibid.

41. White interview.

42. R. Smith interview.

43. Carlson interview.

44. Dexter Filkins, "Volunteer Nurses Go Door-to-door in S. Dade," *Miami Herald,* September 6, 1992.

45. McGill interview.

46. Ponton interview.

47. Ibid.

48. "Jehovah's Witness Hurricane Andrew Relief," mimeographed report, September 21, 1992.

49. Ponton interview.

50. R. Smith interview.

51. Moose interview.

52. Ibid.

53. Ashley interview.

54. Kong interview.

55. Interview with Carolyn Donaldson conducted by Marva Donaldson, December 5, 1992, Miami.

56. Interview with Tony Sardinas conducted by Monica Oliva, November 29, 1992, Miami.

57. Interview with an anonymous worker at Florida Power and Light Company conducted by Monica Y. Oliver, November 16, 1992, Miami (henceforth FPL worker interview).

58. Interview with Melinda Smith conducted by Bob Warzeski, October 24, 1992, Coconut Grove, FL (henceforth M. Smith interview).

59. Ronnie Greene and Marilyn Garateix, "Relief Team Sets Up Tent Cities at Three Sites in Homestead," *Miami Herald*, August 30, 1992.

60. Fran Brennan and Lizette Alvarez, "Tent City Seen as Last Resort," *Miami Herald*, September 3, 1992.

61. Interview with Amy Moss conducted by Eugene F. Provenzo Jr., September 1, 1992, Homestead, Fla.

62. Michael Browning, "Life in Tent City: An Indignity, a Salvation," *Miami Herald*, September 27, 1992.

63. Brennan and Alvarez, "Tent City."

Chapter 5. The First Weeks

1. Granados interview.

2. Interview with Bonnie Sheil conducted by Lesley Sevastopoulos, December 1, 1992, Miami.

3. Baldwin interview.

4. L. Jeffers interview.

5. Brescher interview.

6. M. Smith interview.

7. Kong interview.

8. Interview with Patricia Whitely conducted by Rebecca Hoffman, November 18, 1992, Miami (henceforth Whitely interview).

9. Foote interview.

10. Graham interview.

11. Interview with James P. McCoy conducted by Alisa Moeller, November 7, 1992, Miami.

12. White interview.

13. Carlson interview.

14. Martinez interview.

15. M. Smith interview.

16. Baldwin interview.

17. Ibid.

18. Whitely interview.

19. Interview with Lauren Markoff conducted by Ursula M. Flecha, November 17, 1992, Miami (henceforth Markoff interview).

20. McNanamy interview.

21. Ibid.

22. Susan Trausch, "Hurricane Profiteers: Have We Got a Great Deal for You!" *Miami Herald*, September 8, 1992.

23. John Dorschnei, "The Hurricane that Changed Everything," *Miami Herald*, August 30, 1992.

24. Jones interview

25. Tang interview.

26. Christine Evans, Anne Bartlett, and Scott Higham, "Dade Prices: Rocketing Skyward," *Miami Herald*, August 27, 1992.

27. Graham interview.

28. Grace Lim, "Sharpshooters Targeting Monkeys," *Miami Herald*, August 31, 1992.

29. Rachel Swarns, "Shattered Traffic Lights Leave Drivers Honking," *Miami Herald*, August 27, 1992.

30. "Andrew, Recovery by the Numbers," *Miami Herald*, August 24, 1994.

31. Dan Holly, "Andrew Forces Bureaucrats to Throw the Rules out the Window," *Miami Herald*, August 29, 1992.

32. Interview with Muhammed Mukhtar Hasan conducted by Hafsa Dandia, November 22, 1992, Miami.

33. Martinez interview.

34. Holly, "Andrew Forces Bureaucrats."

35. Richard Wallace, "Sign of the Times," *Miami Herald*, April 27, 1993.

36. Tom Fiedler, "Storm Drives Home the Need for Leadership," *Miami Herald*, August 30, 1992.

37. Ibid.

38. Dexter Filkins, "Mayor Clark Is Calling It Quits," *Miami Herald*, January 26, 1993.

39. Karen Branch, "Hurricane: The Priority Is Help for the Battered Cities," *Miami Herald*, January 31, 1993.

40. Foote interview.

41. Interview with Jeffrey R. Jenkins conducted by Tresca L. Whitehead-Jenkins, April 18, 1993, Miami (henceforth Jenkins interview).

42. Ponton interview.

43. Tom Dubocq, "FPL Fields a Repair Army," *Miami Herald,* August 29, 1992.

44. Alfonso Chardy, "Scavengers Steal Power Lines, Other FPL Equipment to Sell," *Miami Herald,* September 10, 1992.

45. FPL worker interview.

46. Ibid.

47. Fran Brennan, Todd Hartman, and Martin Merzer, "A Half Year Later: Out of the Storm," *Miami Herald,* February 21, 1993.

48. Ibid.

49. Interview with Suzanne Schorle conducted by Leslie Monreal, November 12, 1992, Miami (henceforth Schorle interview).

50. Lizette Alvarez, "Organized Tent City Proposed," *Miami Herald,* December 19, 1992.

51. Rachel L. Swarns, "For Some, Tent City Is a Veritable Paradise," *Miami Herald,* September 6,1992.

52. Interview with Malcolm Kahn conducted by Cynthia Reed, December 6, 1992, Miami (henceforth Kahn interview).

53. Whitely interview.

54. Laskis interview.

55. Laughlin interview.

56. Markoff interview.

57. Interview with LaWanda Scott conducted by Ursula M. Flecha, November 20, 1992, Miami (henceforth Scott interview).

58. Mooney interview.

59. Ashley interview.

60. Interview with Claudia Shukat conducted by Karen G. Befeler-Neuhaus, November 14, 1992, Miami (henceforth Shukat interview).

61. Johnson interview.

62. Baljet interview.

63. Ashley interview.

Chapter 6. Rebuilding the Community

1. Anne Bartlett, "Concertgoers Are Urged to Arrive Early," *Miami Herald,* September 26, 1992.

2. Interview with Gabriel Gabor conducted by Barbara Jaimes, March 22, 1993, Miami.

3. Ibid.

4. Interview with Saribel Ceballos conducted by Elise Belaga, December 3, 1992, Miami.

5. Brent Mitchell, "Hurricane-displaced Disabled Make Best of Less-Homey Home," *Miami Herald,* December 31, 1992, Neighbors Section, 15. Mitchell reported that eight months after the hurricane, little or no progress had been made in rebuilding the group homes run by Miami Cerebral Palsy in the Goulds area. Only

$200,000 of the $1.6 million needed to rebuild had been donated. Total funds needed to complete the project were estimated at $8 million.

6. Peggy Rogers, "Disabled Group Suffers from Move After Storm," *Miami Herald,* April 20, 1993.

7. Interview with Blake Bergman conducted by Elise Belaga, November 20, 1992, Miami.

8. Ibid.

9. White interview.

10. Mooney interview.

11. Moose interview.

12. David Hancock, "Environmentalists Urge Halt to Debris Burning," *Miami Herald,* September 8, 1992.

13. Interview with Harold Wanless conducted by Robert Warzeski, December 3, 1992, Miami (henceforth Wanless interview).

14. Ibid.

15. Ibid.

16. Ibid.

17. Curtis Morgan and Cyril T. Zaneski, "Resilience of Glades Put to Test," *Miami Herald,* September 8, 1992.

18. Wanless interview.

19. Fran Brennan and David Hancock, "Despair in the Fields," *Miami Herald,* August 27, 1992.

20. Interview with Pablo E. Perez, November 27, 1992, Miami; interviewer unidentified.

21. Ibid.

22. Marilyn Adams, "Nurseryman's Plants Wiped Out by the Storm," *Miami Herald,* September 5, 1992.

23. James McNair, "Farm Losses Tallied at $1.04 Billion," *Miami Herald,* September 10, 1992.

24. John Donnelly, "Hurricane Ushers in Year of the Rat," *Miami Herald,* March 27, 1993.

25. Anderson interview.

26. Baldwin interview.

27. David Kidwell, "On the Rebound," *Miami Herald,* January 22, 1993.

28. Cindy Ycaza, "Monkey Jungle Set to Reopen Dec. 5," *Miami Herald,* November 22, 1992, Neighbors Section, 36.

29. Interview with John Frosbutter conducted by Karen Heil, December 7, 1992, Miami.

30. David Satterfield, "Tourists Finding Attractions Slowly Reopening Doors," *Miami Herald,* November 29, 1992.

31. Interview with Richard B. Howard conducted by Ana Maria Tejeda, December 4, 1992, Miami, Florida (henceforth Howard interview).

32. Feldman interview.

33. *Toucan Talk Extra* 18, 5 and 6 (December 1992): 1.

34. John Donnelly, "The Rebuilt Metrozoo Ready to Roar Once More," *Miami Herald*, December 16, 1992.

35. *Toucan Talk Extra*, 1, 3.

36. Kong interview.

37. Ibid.

38. Ibid.

39. *Toucan Talk Extra*, 26. Naomi Browning was killed by a beam that fell on her in her bedroom.

40. Todd Hartman, "Metrozoo's Reopening Crowded," *Miami Herald*, December 19, 1992.

41. Richard Wallace, "Visitors Slow to Return," *Miami Herald*, January 29, 1993.

42. Anne Moncreiff Arrarte, "South Dade at Retail Crossroads," *Miami Herald*, September 5, 1992.

43. Anthony Faiola, "Bonanza in South Dade," *Miami Herald*, January 23, 1993.

44. Ibid.

45. "Andrew, Recovery by the Numbers."

46. David Satterfield and Mark Silva, "State Ready to Tackle Dade's Insurance Crisis," *Miami Herald*, December 6, 1992.

47. Ibid.

48. Shukat interview.

49. Ibid.

50. Ibid.

51. Ibid.

52. Interview with Juan Hernandez (pseudonym) conducted by Raquel Fundora, December 1, 1992, Miami.

53. Ibid.

54. Fred Tasker, "Hurricane Andrew and Ethics," *Miami Herald*, January 10, 1992.

55. Ibid., "Victims? Check the Mirror," *Miami Herald*, January 10, 1993.

56. Deborah Sharp, "In South Florida Raising the Roof and the Crime Rate," *USA Today*, February 15, 1993, 3A.

57. Interview with Dan Stokes conducted by Lauren Markoff, April 26, 1993, Miami (henceforth Stokes interview).

58. Ibid.

59. Ibid.

60. Ibid.

61. Interview with Nora Porobic conducted by Rachel Szlegier, April 21, 1993, Miami.

62. Stokes interview.

63. Todd Hartman, "Hurricane Season Brought Lessons Home," *Miami Herald*, December 1, 1992.

64. Jeff Leen, Stephen K. Doig, and Lisa Getter, "Failure of Design and Discipline," *Miami Herald*, December 20, 1992.

65. Ibid.

66. Norcross interview.

67. Ibid.

68. Pernick interview.

69. Ibid.

70. Ibid.

71. Jenkins interview.

72. Pernick interview.

73. David Satterfield, "Pulling Up Stakes: Thousands Planning to Relocate Because of Andrew," *Miami Herald*, November 10, 1992.

74. Fran Brennan, "Many Vowing to Walk Away from the Lives They Built," *Miami Herald*, August 28, 1992.

75. Peter Slavin, "3 Months Later, Lives Still on Edge," *Miami Herald*, November 24, 1992.

76. Larry Birger, "Northward Migration Benefits Weston," *Miami Herald*, December 25, 1992.

77. Editorial, "Metro Winks, Andrew Sinks," *Miami Herald*, November 10, 1992.

78. Shaffer interview.

79. Ibid.

80. Ibid.

81. Granados interview.

82. Jenkins interview.

83. Kong interview.

84. Interview with Allen Farrington conducted by Rachel Szlegier, April 14, 1993, Miami.

85. A. Jeffers interview.

86. L. Jeffers interview.

87. Todd Hartman, "Homestead Habitat Builds on Volunteer Spirit," *Miami Herald*, November 26, 1992, Neighbors Section, 10.

88. Lizette Alvarez, "Habitat Hammering Away to Reach Target," *Miami Herald*, February 8, 1993.

89. Interview with Betty Holmes conducted by Lynne Katz, November 17, 1992, Miami.

90. Ibid.

91. Ibid.

92. Ibid.

93. John Donnelly, "Rebuild Group OKs Major Housing Funds," *Miami Herald*, March 3, 1993. The We Will Rebuild Campaign was led by Alvah Chapman, then CEO of Knight-Ridder Publications. The foundation raised over $30 million for use in rebuilding the community and subsequently created and endowed the International Hurricane Center at Florida International University.

94. Alfonso Chardy, "Air Force Base Families Have Bitter Homecoming," *Miami Herald*, August 29, 1992.

95. Todd Hartman and Patrick May, "Gloom over Homestead," *Miami Herald,* March 13, 1993.

96. Rachel Swarns, "Family Bonds Battered," *Miami Herald,* January 3, 1993.

97. Lizette Alvarez, "Experts: Storm Survivors Suffer Combat Symptoms, " *Miami Herald,* January 9, 1993.

98. Fran Brennan, "Homestead's Heartfelt March," *Miami Herald,* January 21, 1993.

99. Ibid., "Marching on Washington," *Miami Herald,* January 24, 1992, Neighbors Section, 26.

100. Brandon interview.

101. Ibid.

102. Ibid.

Chapter 7. Life Will Never Be the Same

1. Lydia Martin, "Coming Home to a Strange Place," *Miami Herald,* November 27, 1992.

2. Ibid.

3. Slevin, "3 Months Later."

4. Carney interview.

5. Schorle interview.

6. Camner interview.

7. Warren interview.

8. Scott interview.

9. Carlson interview.

10. Dee interview.

11. Carlson interview.

12. Kahn interview.

13. White interview.

14. Jones interview.

15. Tang interview.

16. Howard interview.

17. Foote interview.

18. Brandon interview.

19. Ashley interview.

20. Ana Veciana-Suarez, "Memories of Terror, Despair, Destruction Won't Go Away," *Miami Herald,* August 22, 1993.

21. Ibid., "As Normalcy Returns, Hurricane's Lessons Seem Dust in the Wind," *Miami Herald,* August 21, 1994.

Appendix A

Participants in the Hurricane Andrew
Oral History Research Project

Pamela E. Abbey

Karen G. Befeler-Neuhaus

Elise Belaga

Bruce Bentley

Lori Burnstine

Jennifer Caunedo

Lyn Culbertson

Dan Dalke

Hasfa Dandia

Marva Donaldson

Joan Dudas

Ursula M. Flecha

Raquel Fundora

Denise Goldstein

Jill Goldston

Lori Guarini

Juliet E. Hart

Karen Heil

Rebecca A. Hoffman

Billie Houston

A retail store in the Cutler Ridge Mall, north of Homestead, destroyed by Hurricane Andrew. (Image ID: wea00551)

Barbara Jaimes-Quero

Dan Jenkins

Leshawn Jones

Lynne Katz

Mykel Mangrum

Lauren Markoff

Alisa M. Moeller

Leslie Monreal

Monica Y. Oliva

Allen C. Paul

Asterie Baker Provenzo

Eugene F. Provenzo Jr.

Beatriz Quintairos

Cynthia Reed

Ana Maria Rego

Erika Sardi

Lesley Sevastopoulos

Eric Shane

Sally A. Shay

Deborah Strand

Rachel Szlegier

Anna Maria Tejada

Bob E. Warzeshy

Tresca L. Whitehead-Jenkins

Ginger Williams

Appendix B

Bibliography of Writings on Hurricane Andrew

Compiled by William E. Brown, Jr.

Hurricane Andrew touched land in South Florida on August 24, 1992. This bibliography, originally published in the *Bulletin of Bibliography* to mark the fifth anniversary of that cataclysmic event, is updated and expanded for inclusion in this volume and appears with the permission of the editors of the *Bulletin*. For residents of the South Florida region and many more across the Gulf Coast of the United States, particularly coastal residents of Louisiana and Texas, Hurricane Andrew remains a vivid memory. Each of us who survived Hurricane Andrew and its aftermath will always view the episode as a signature event in our lives. We will carry with us an unforgettable array of personal memories, some good, some

An F-16 outside a wind-damaged repair shop at Homestead Air Force Base. (Image ID: weaoo560)

bad. As time marches on, however, the human mind allows us to develop a necessary distance from such a traumatic event. As this bibliography indicates, the historical legacy of Andrew is assured, and future generations will be able to consult a wealth of published information on this natural disaster. In fact, few natural disasters can claim such an extensive body of published work.

To date, more than three hundred books, pamphlets, and conference proceedings; local, state, and federal government reports; video recordings and documentaries; planning and recovery studies and environmental investigations; and pictorial works, maps, novels, and other publications are available from private publishers, government agencies, local media outlets, educational institutions, and libraries. In addition, graduate students across the United States have prepared approximately fifty dissertations on various aspects of Hurricane Andrew. This mountain of information offers a dramatic window onto the enormous emotional, physical, environmental, political, financial, and cultural impact of Hurricane Andrew. And this impressive list of materials does not begin to take into account the scores of newspaper and magazine stories, television and radio reports, research journal articles, and other narratives produced during the past five years.

A search for published accounts of the famous Florida Hurricane of 1926 located only five noteworthy pamphlets and publications on this terrible storm. In retrospect, there seemed to be that many pictorial histories and video documentaries on Andrew available before the Miami-area traffic lights were back in working order. Of course, 1926 and 1992 represent two vastly different eras in South Florida, and our capacity to both create and consume documents and images on natural disasters is far greater today.

The published writings about Andrew are not, after all, primarily for you and me. They serve as an important part of the historical record. These books, reports, pamphlets, and other materials join with our spoken words and haunting images to capture a landmark event in our community.

Both individual authors and local media issued pictorial histories of Andrew in the weeks following the storm. In South Florida, area newspapers including the *Miami Herald, El Nuevo Herald,* the *Sun-Sentinel,* and the *Palm Beach Post* were among the first to generate pictorial publications. Local television stations rushed video documentaries to a market thirsty for the words and images of survivors, disaster recovery volunteers, local, state, and national political figures, and news media members themselves. Modern-day printing and publishing technology helped feed the local and national demand for works on Andrew, and many of these works were produced outside the decimated South Florida region in the days and weeks following the storm.

A group of conference reports and proceedings appeared in print during the months following Andrew. An "environmental summit" sponsored by the Redland Conservancy; "Lessons Learned from Hurricane Andrew," hosted by Florida International University; excerpts from the Fifteenth Annual National Hurricane Conference (1993), "A New South Dade Planning Charette," and a symposium that reviewed the impact of Andrew and Iniki, a hurricane that struck Hawaii that same year, are some of the gatherings that generated publications. An abundance of state and federal publications now fills the bookshelves of libraries, government offices, schools, and related agencies. Works analyze storm damage; offer recovery advice; provide insurance tips; evaluate disaster plans and relief efforts; investigate environmental effects on water levels, plants, animals, coastal areas, off-shore pipelines, and coral reefs; explore storm-surge phenomena; review relocation and reconstruction efforts; study insurance company behavior; and review building-code requirements.

Two noteworthy books on Andrew—Howard Kleinberg's *The Florida Hurricane and Disaster, 1992,* and Eugene F. Provenzo and Sandra H. Fradd's *Hurricane Andrew, the Public Schools, and the Rebuilding of Community*—also proved fertile ground for graduate student dissertations, and students at the University of Miami, and across the nation, have produced an eclectic and important body of work. Many dissertations explore crucial issues relating to public health, children's physical and mental health, the natural environmental; interpersonal relationships, and disaster planning and recovery efforts. A detailed study on population dynamics and mating systems are the focus of one study; the paper's subject matter, however, is not human beings but the tropical understory shrub *Ardisia escallonioides* (Myrsinaceae).

No natural disaster is complete without the publication of fictionalized accounts of terror and heroism. Hurricane Andrew is portrayed in at least one novel, Heather Graham Pozzessere's *The Trouble with Andrew,* a forgettable romance novel that places the main characters in the midst of the storm's savage conditions. This work joins a more substantive body of fictional works on South Florida hurricanes, including Marjory Stoneman Douglas's *Hurricane* (1976), Carl Hiaasen's *Stormy Weather* (1995), and Henry Stansbury's *Hurricane in the Keys: A Novel about Seeding Hurricanes and a Vivid History of the Keys* (1968).

General

Adams, Charles M. *The Effect of Hurricane Andrew on Monroe County Businesses: Negative Economic Effects and Assistance Sought.* Gainesville: Food and Resource Economics Department, Institute of Food and Agricultural Sciences, University of Florida, 1995. 36 pp.

After the Hurricane: A Guide to Restoring Rural Housing and Communities in Florida. Washington, D.C.: The Council, 1992. 21 pp.

After the Hurricane: A Guide to Restoring Housing in Rural Louisiana. Washington, D.C.: The Council, 1992. 42 pp.

Ahmadi-Nedushan, Behrooz. "Progressive Collapse Analysis of Offshore Platforms." Master's thesis, McGill University, 1995. 162 pp.

Alguire, Hal K. *USA, CE, Deputy District Oral History Interview with Major Hal K. Alguire Engineer.* [Jacksonville]: The District, 1994. 41 leaves.

Alvarez, Leonardo, Jorge Hernandez, Cathy Leff, and Daniel Williams, eds. *The New South Dade Planning Charette: From Adversity to Opportunity.* [Miami]: Innovation Committee of We Will Rebuild, c. 1992. 11 pp.

American Institute of Biological Sciences. *Hurricane Andrew's Sweep Through Natural Ecosystems: BioScience.* Washington, D.C.: American Institute of Biological Sciences, 1994.

Ames, Laura Theresa. "Content Analysis of the Newspaper Coverage of Hurricane Andrew." Master's thesis, University of Miami, 1996. 45 leaves.

An Act Making Supplemental Appropriations, Transfers, and Rescissions for the Fiscal Year Ending September 30, 1992, and for Other Purposes. Washington D.C.: GPO, 1992. 46 pp.

Anclade, Cathy. "Dealing with Disaster: The Importance of Preparedness—The South Florida Waste Management District Felt the Full Fury of Hurricane Andrew." *Government Finance Review* 8, 6 (December 1992). 11 pp.

A Study of the Psychology Effects of Hurricane Andrew on an Elementary School Population. Boulder: Natural Hazards Research and Applications Information Center, University of Colorado, 1993. 88 pp.

Applied Geography Conferences. *Papers and Proceedings of the Applied Geography Conferences.* 16th conference. Toronto, Ontario, 1993. 174 pp.

Bailey, William E. *Andrew's Legacy : The Winds of Change.* West Palm Beach: Telshare Publishing, 1999. 197 pp.

Bair, Frank E. *Hurricane Andrew: Storm of the Century: A Pictorial Review of America's Most Destructive Storm Ever.* Fort Lauderdale: Dade Book, 1992. 99 pp.

Baker, Edward K. *Analysis of Hurricane Andrew Economic Damage and Recovery Options for the Boating, Marina, and Marine Service Industries.* Gainesville: Florida Sea Grant College Program, University of Florida, 1993. 100 pp.

Baumann, Bette. *Hurricane Andrew: The Big One.* Longboat Key, Fla.: MetroMedia Marketing, 1992. 56 pp.

Beatley, Timothy. *Hazard Mitigation in Florida Following Hurricane Andrew.* Chapel Hill: Center for Urban and Regional Studies, University of North Carolina, 1997. 61 pp.

Bhinderwal, Shiraj. "Insurance Loss Analysis of Single Family Dwellings Damaged in Hurricane Andrew." Master's thesis, Clemson University, 1995. 74 leaves.

Bischof, Barbel G. "Aerial Photographic Analysis of Coastal and Estuarine Mangrove System Dynamics of the Everglades National Park, Florida, in Response to Hurricanes: Implications for the Continuing Sealevel Rise." Master's thesis, University of Miami, 1995. 151 leaves.

Borden, Jill Marie. "Use of a Macroalgal Functional-Form Model to Assess Disturbance Impacts on a Coral Reef." Master's thesis, University of Miami, 1995. 90 leaves.

Butler, Howard K. *U.S. Army Aviation and Troop Command Support to Task Force Andrew, 1992.* Washington, D.C.: GPO, 1993. 75 pp.

Carley, Kathleen. *Hurricane Andrew: Organizing for Response—Comparing Practice, Plan, and Theory.* [Boulder]: Natural Hazards Research and Applications Center, University of Colorado, 1993. 30 pp.

Carroll, Dale A. *The Role of the U.S. Army Medical Department in Domestic Disaster Assistance Operations: Lessons Learned from Hurricane Andrew.* Carlisle Barracks, Pa.: U.S. Army War College, 1996. 41 pp.

Catlett-Newby, Vicky L. "The Effects of Evacuation and Relocation Following Hurricane Andrew on Children Ages Two Through Six." Ph.D. diss., Florida International University, 1993. 220 leaves.

Center for Urban Transportation Research. *The Impact of Hurricane Andrew on Tri-Rail Ridership.* Tampa: Center for Urban Transportation Research, University of South Florida, 1993. 41 pp.

Chite, Ralph. *Hurricane Andrew Agricultural Losses and Available Federal Assistance.* [Washington, D.C.]: Congressional Research Service, Library of Congress, 1992. 6 pp.

Chung, Joon-Hai. "The 'Flight to Quality,' Global Capacity, and the United States Reinsurance Prices." Ph.D. diss., Temple University, 1999. 117 pp.

Coastal Education and Research Foundation. *Impacts of Hurricane Andrew on the*

Coastal Zones of Florida and Louisiana, 22–26 August 1992. Fort Lauderdale: Coastal Education and Research Foundation, 1995. 364 pp.

Coastal Technology Corporation. *Effects of Hurricane Andrew on Dade County's Artificial Reefs, Florida*. Vero Beach, Fla.: Coastal Technology Corporation, 1993. 17 pp.

Colmenares, Nicholas Francisco. "Hazard Migration in South Florida: Evaluating the Risks to Regional Sustainable Development." Ph.D. diss., University of Colorado at Boulder, 1997. 428 pp.

Cone, Deborah L. "Post-Hurricane Needs in Individuals One Year Later." Master's thesis, Barry University, 1994. 43 leaves.

Cook, Ronald A. *Hurricane Andrew: Recommendations for Building Codes and Building Code Enforcement: Final Report*. Gainesville: University of Florida, 1993.

Costello, Nancy Lorraine. "Emotional Expression and Trauma: Relationships to Optimism, Coping, Neuroendocrine, and Immune System Functioning." Ph.D. diss., University of Miami, 1997. 399 pp.

Cruess, Dean G. "Psychoneuroendocrine Response to Posttraumatic Stress among Men Following Hurricane Andrew." Master's thesis, University of Miami, 1996. 115 leaves.

Cuban American National Foundation. *Hurricane Andrew Relief Effort, August/September 1992*. Miami: Cuban American National Foundation, 1992.

Culp, Janet F. *Effects of Hurricane Andrew on Water Levels in Coastal Florida and Louisiana Data Report*. Rockville, Md.: U.S. Department of Commerce, 1992.

Current, Carole Louise. "Spectral Model Simulation of Wind-Driven Subinertial Circulation on the Inner Texas Louisiana Shelf." Ph.D. diss, Texas A&M University, 1996. 144 pp.

Curtis, Thom. "Child Abuse in the Wake of Natural Disasters." Ph.D. diss., Utah State University, 1995. 200 pp.

Daniels, Gerald R. *Hurricane Andrew's Impact on Natural Gas and Oil Facilities on the Outer Continental Shelf, Interim Report, as of November 1993*. Herndon, Va.: U.S. Department of the Interior, 1994. 49 pp.

Davis, Ellen Rachael. "Predicting Posttraumatic Phenomena in Children with Anxiety Disorder Following Hurricane Andrew: A Test of a Conceptual Model." Ph.D. diss., University of Miami, 1995. 145 leaves.

Disaster Management, Inc. *Disaster Plan: Business Continuation Plan: Hurricanes, Tornadoes, Fires, Winter Storms, Floods, Thunder, and Lightning*. [Miami]: Disaster Management, 1994.

———. *Disaster Plan: Human Resource Plan: Hurricane Andrew, NWS Radar, August 24 1992*. [Miami]: Disaster Management, 1994.

Dynes, Russell Rowe. *FEMA: Disaster Relief or Disaster Period?* Newark: Disaster Research Center, University of Delaware, 1992. 11 leaves.

EQE International. *Hurricanes Andrew and Iniki, 1992*. San Francisco: EQE International, 1992. 8 pp.

Evangeline Economic and Planning District. *Hurricane Andrew: A Strategy for Eco-*

nomic Recovery. [Lafayette, La.]: Evangeline Economic and Planning District, 1994. 44 leaves.

Eyerdam, Rick. *When Natural Disaster Strikes: Lessons from Hurricane Andrew.* Miami Beach: Hospice Foundation of America, 1994. 134 pp.

Federal Emergency Management Agency. *Andrew, Iniki, Omar: FEMA Evaluation of Federal Response and Recovery Efforts.* Washington, D.C.: Federal Emergency Management Agency, 1993. 88 pp.

————. *FEMA's Disaster Management Program: A Performance Audit after Hurricane Andrew.* Washington, D.C.: Federal Emergency Management Agency, 1993. 206 pp.

————. *Interagency Hazard Mitigation Team Report: In Response to the August 24, 1992, Disaster Declaration for the State of Florida . . . Hurricane Andrew.* Atlanta: Federal Emergency Management Agency Disaster Assistance Programs Region IV, 1992. 174 pp.

Federal Insurance Administration. *Building Performance: Hurricane Andrew in Florida—Observations, Recommendations, and Technical Guidance.* Washington D.C.: Federal Emergency Management Agency, 1992.

Fiorino, Steven Thomas. "On the Origins of Low-Level Tornadic Circulations Within the Remnants of Hurricane Andrew." Master's thesis, Ohio State University, 1993. 66 leaves.

Fisher, David E. *The Scariest Place on Earth: Eye to Eye with Hurricanes.* New York: Random House, 1994. 250 pp.

Fisher, Jack B. *Final Report on U.S. Fish and Wildlife Service Grant Agreement 1448-0004-93-924.* [Atlanta]: U.S. Fish and Wildlife Service, 1995. 6 leaves.

Florida Department of Insurance. "Are You Prepared? A Hurricane Checklist for Insurance Consumers." Tallahassee: Florida Department of Insurance, 1993. 1 sheet. (Also in Spanish: "Esta a preparado Pra el Proximo Huracan? Lista para los Consumidores de Seguros.")

————. *Hurricane Andrew's Impact on Insurance in the State of Florida.* Tallahassee: Florida Department of Insurance, 1993. 38 pp.

Florida Office of Program Policy Analysis and Government Accountability. *Review of the Post-Disaster Relocation and Reconstruction.* [Tallahassee]: Florida Office of Program Policy Analysis and Government Accountability, 1996. 4 pp.

Florida Office of the Governor. *Hurricane Andrew in Florida.* [Tallahassee]: Office of the Governor, 1993. 12 pp.

Florida Sea Grant College Program. *Location and Assessment of Hurricane Andrew–Damaged Vessels on Biscayne Bay and Adjoining Shore Areas.* Gainesville: Florida Sea Grant College Program, University of Florida, 1993. 12 pp.

Florida Study Commission on Property Insurance and Reinsurance. *Report of the Study Commission on Property Insurance and Reinsurance.* [Tallahassee]: State of Florida, 1993.

Flott, Phyllis L. "An Analysis of the Determinants of Recovery after a Natural Disaster

Using a Multi-Paradigm Approach." Ph.D. diss., University of North Texas, 1996. 270 pp.

Fort Lauderdale Sun-Sentinel staff. *Andrew! Savagery from the Sea, August 24, 1992.* Orlando: Tribune, 1992. 92 pp.

Gant, Diana. "The Web of Affiliation: Theoretical Motives for the Strategic Establishment of Inter-Organizational Relationships of the World Wide Web." Ph.D. diss., Carnegie-Mellon University, 1998. 154 pp.

Gore, Rick. *Andrew Aftermath.* [Washington, D.C.]: National Geographic Society, 1993.

Gorham, Lance Elliott. "Impacts of Periodic and Catastrophic Disturbance on the Plant and Terrestrial Invertebrate Communities of Wetland Forests." Ph.D. diss., University of Southwestern Louisiana, 1999. 114 pp.

Governor's Disaster Planning and Response Review Committee. *Final Report.* Tallahassee: Governor's Disaster Planning and Response Review Committee, 1993. 89 pp.

Guarisco, Tom. *Hurricane Andrew: A Diary of Destruction in South Louisiana, August 26, 1992.* Lubbock, Tex.: C. F. Boone, 1992. 64 pp.

Guillette, Elizabeth A. *The Role of the Aged in Community Recovery Following Hurricane Andrew.* Boulder: Natural Hazards Research and Applications Information Center, University of Colorado, 1993. 5 pp.

Guntenspergen, Glenn R. *Winds: Hurricane Andrew and Louisiana's Coast.* Lafayette, La.: National Biological Service, Southern Science Center, 1996. 16 pp.

Hamann, Richard G. *Mitigation of Hurricane Losses: Federal, State, and Local Programs.* Gainesville: Florida Sea Grant College Program, University of Florida, 1990. 231 pp.

Hart, Robert M. "Changing Winds: The Role of Military Public Affairs in Press Coverage of Hurricane Andrew." Master's thesis, University of Florida, 1995. 86 leaves.

Harvey, Mitchell Neal. "Analysis and Evaluation of Hurricane Preparedness Planning in Dade County, Florida." Master's thesis, University of Miami, 1980. 120 leaves.

Hebdon, F. J. *Effect of Hurricane Andrew on the Turkey Point Nuclear Generating Station from August 20–30, 1992.* Washington, D.C., and Springfield, Va.: [The commission]; 1993, 28 pp.

Hubscher, Dennis J. *Homestead AFB after Hurricane Andrew—Whether to Rebuild or Not: A Critique on Base Closures and Public Decisionmaking.* Washington, D.C.: Industrial College of the Armed Forces, National Defense University, 1993.

Hurricane! A Familiarization Booklet. New Orleans: U.S. Army Engineer District, 1993. 56 pp.

Hurricane! The Rage of Hurricane Andrew. Milwaukee: Gareth Stevens, 1993. 48 pp.

Hurricane Andrew: Images from the Killer Storm. Marietta, Ga.: Longstreet Press, 1992. 96 pp.

Hurricane Andrew: Path of Destruction, August 1992. Charleston, S.C.: Historic Publications, 1992. 98 pp.

Hurricane Andrew Recovery and Rebuilding Trust Fund, Vocational Training, and Employment Services Program. [Miami]: BTVTC, 1993.

Impact of Hurricane Andrew on Performance, Interaction, and Recovery of Lifelines. EQE International; Thomas Larsen et al.; San Francisco, Calif.: EQE International, 1996.

Insurance Institute for Property Loss Reduction. *Coastal Exposure and Community Protection: Hurricane Andrew's Legacy.* Wheaton, Ill., and Boston, Mass.: Insurance Institute for Property Loss Reduction, 1995. 48 pp.

Jacobs, Dennis M. *Forest Resource Damage Assessment of Hurricane Andrew in Southern Louisiana Using Airborne Videography.* New Orleans: U.S. Forest Service, U.S. Dept of Agriculture, 1994. 9 pp.

Jeans, Deborah. *A Practical Guide to Ferret Care.* Miami: Privately published, 1994. 146 pp.

Keith, Edward L. *Hurricane Andrew: Structural Performance of Buildings in Southern Florida (August 24, 1992).* Tacoma: American Plywood Association, 1992. 77 pp.

Kilbourn, Kristin Michelle. "The Effects of Hurricane Andrew on Coping, Distress, Immune, and Endocrine Factors in a Group of HIV+ Gay Men." Ph.D. diss., University of Miami, 1996. 240 pp.

Kleinberg, Howard. *The Florida Hurricane and Disaster, 1992.* (Includes *The Florida Hurricane and Disaster,* by L. F. Reardon, reprint of 1926 ed.) Miami: Centennial Press, 1992. 88 pp., 122 pp.

Kraus, Laurie Ann. "Rebuilding the Walls: A Narrative-Theological Model for Disaster Relief in the Wake of Hurricane Andrew." Master's thesis, Columbia Theological Seminary, 1994. 144 leaves.

La Ira de los Vientos: el Huracan Andrew. Kansas City, Mo.: Andrews and McMeel, 1992. 160 pp.

Lehman, Jessica M. "Coping with Chronic Illness and Hurricane Andrew and Its Relationship to Symptoms, Immune Function, and Illness Burden in Chronic Fatigue Syndrome." Master's thesis, University of Miami, 1996. 47 leaves.

Levy, Louis J. *Improving Disaster Planning and Response Efforts: Lessons from Hurricanes Andrew and Iniki.* N.p.: Booz-Allen & Hamilton, 1993. 48 pp.

Louisiana Department of Agriculture and Forestry. Urban Forestry Program. *Hurricane Resistant Landscapes: Preparing the Landscape to Withstand Hurricane Storms.* [Baton Rouge]: Louisiana Department of Agriculture and Forestry, 1994. 8 pp.

Lovelace, John K. *Storm-tide Elevations Produced by Hurricane Andrew along the Louisiana Coast, August 25–27, 1992.* Baton Rouge, La.: U.S. Geological Survey, 1994. 45 pp.

Lyskowski, Roman, and Steve Rice, eds. *The Big One: Hurricane Andrew.* Kansas City, Mo.: Andrews and McMeel, 1992. 160 pp.

Mandke, J. S. *Evaluation of Hurricane-Induced Damage to Offshore Pipelines.* Washington, D.C.: U.S. Department of the Interior, 1995. 3 pp.

Mann, Philip H., ed. *Lessons Learned from Hurricane Andrew: A Conference Sponsored by Florida International University.* Miami: Florida International University, 1993. 196 pp.

Mayfield, Max. *Atlantic Hurricanes.* Washington, D.C.: Heldref Publications, 1993. 9 pp.

Mayo, Kevin E. "An Information Visualization of Hurricane Andrew's Track across South Florida, August 23–24, 1992." Master's thesis, Florida Atlantic University, 1998. 57 leaves.

Mazurek, D. F. "Report of Investigation of COMMSTA MIAMI, 300–ft. Guyed Towers Which Collapsed during Hurricane Andrew." New London, Conn.: Center for Advanced Studies, U.S. Coast Guard Academy, 1992.

McDonnell, Janet A. *Hurricane Andrew: Historical Report.* Fort Belvoir, Va.: U.S. Army Corps of Engineers, 1993. 69 pp.

Meier, Ouida Diane Williams. "A Long-Term Study of Reef Coral Dynamics in the Florida Keys." Ph.D. diss., University of Georgia, 1996. 230 pp.

Metropolitan Dade County. *Hurricane Andrew Recovery Status Report, June 18, 1993.* Miami: Metro-Dade County, 1993.

———. Office of Emergency Management. *Dade County Evacuation Order.* Miami: Metro-Dade County, 1992. 12 pp.

Miami Herald staff. *Hurricanes: How to Prepare and Recover.* Kansas City, Mo.: Andrews and McMeel, 1993. 125 pp.

Misra, Vasubandhu. "A Statistically Based Cumulus Parameterization Scheme that Makes Use of Heating and Moistening Rates Derived from Observations." Ph.D. diss., Florida State University, 1997. 186 pp.

Mittler, Elliott. *A Case Study of Florida's Homeowners' UE Insurance since Hurricane Andrew.* Boulder: Institute of Behavioral Science, University of Colorado, 1997. http://www.colorado.edu/hazards/wp/wp96.html.

Mumy, Elaine Schoka. "Empathy as Perceived Emotional Social Support among Fire Fighters in Hurricane Andrew." Master's thesis, University of North Texas, 1995. 87 pp.

Murray, Mitchell H. *Storm-Tide Elevations Produced by Hurricane Andrew along the Southern Florida Coasts, August 24, 1992.* Tallahassee, Fla.: U.S. Geological Survey, 1994. 27 pp.

Murray. Peter. *Hurricanes.* Plymouth, Minn.: Child's World, 1996. 30 pp.

National Academy of Public Administration. *Coping with Catastrophe: Building an Emergency Management System to Meet People's Needs in Natural and Manmade Disasters.* Washington D.C.: National Academy of Public Administration, 1993. 133 pp.

Natural Hazards Research and Applications Information Center. *Preliminary Assessment of Damage to Engineered Structures Caused by Hurricane Andrew in Florida.* Boulder, Colo.: Natural Hazards Research and Applications Information Center, 1993. 11 pp.

Nelson, Richard. *Opportunities in the Wake of Hurricane Andrew.* Privately published, 1992. 90 leaves.

Newspaper Articles from the Advocate on Hurricane Andrew Published from Aug. 25, 1992 to Sept. 13, 1992. [Rockville, Md.]: National Oceanic and Atmospheric Administration Central Library, 1993.

Newspaper Articles from the Miami Herald and Nuevo Heraldo on Hurricane Andrew published from Aug. 24, 1992, to Nov. 10, 1992. [Rockville, Md]: National Oceanic and Atmospheric Administration Central Library, 1993.

Parsons, Michael Lewis. "Paleoindicators of Changing Water Conditions in Louisiana Estuaries." Ph.D. diss., Louisiana State University and Agricultural and Mechanical College, 1996. 302 pp.

Pascarella, John Betters. "The Effects of Hurricane Andrew on the Population Dynamics and Mating System of the Tropical Understory Shrub *Ardisia escallonioides* (Myrsinaceae)." Ph.D. diss., University of Miami, 1995. 308 leaves.

Peacock, Walter Gillis, Betty Hearn Morrow, and Hugh Gladwyn, eds. *Hurricane Andrew: Ethnicity, Gender, and the Sociology of Disasters.* London: Routledge, 1997. 277 pp.

Pielke, Roger A. *Hurricane Andrew in South Florida: Mesoscale Weather and Societal Responses.* [Boulder]: National Center for Atmospheric Research, 1995.

Pine, John C. *A Systems View of Emergency Response to Hurricane Andrew.* [Boulder: Natural Hazards Research and Applications Center, University of Colorado], 1993. 12 pp.

Post, Buckley, Schuh, and Jernigan, Inc. *Hurricane Andrew Assessment—Louisiana: Review of Hurricane Evacuation Studies Utilization and Information Dissemination.* Tallahassee: Post, Buckley, Schuh and Jernigan, 1993. 1 vol.

Preston, Edmund. *In Andrew's Path: A Historical Report on FAA's Response to and Recovery from Hurricane Andrew.* Washington, D.C.: U.S. Department of Transportation, 1993. 43 pp.

Prinstein, Mitchell J. "The Children's Coping Assistance Checklist: Examining Types and Sources of Coping Assistance in Children after a Hurricane." Master's thesis, University of Miami, 1994. 83 leaves.

Provenzo, Eugene F., and Sandra H. Fradd. *Hurricane Andrew, the Public Schools, and the Rebuilding of Community.* Albany: State University of New York Press, 1995. 177 pp.

Pruitt, Chris. *Disaster Preparedness and Hurricane Hardening for the Modern Facility: Building Failures of Hurricanes Andrew and Hugo.* West Palm Beach: Gee and Jenson, 1995. 9 [8] pp.

Quraishy, Masud. *Before and After Hurricane Andrew, 1992.* Miami: Kenya Photo Mural, 1992. 96 pp.

Rappaport, Edward N. *Hurricane Andrew: A Preliminary Look.* Washington, D.C.: National Oceanic and Atmospheric Administration, 1992. [10 pp.]

———. *Preliminary Report (Updated 2 March 1993) Hurricane Andrew, 16–28 August 1992.* [Miami]: National Hurricane Center, 1993. 36 pp.

———. *Preliminary Report Hurricane Andrew, 16–28 August 1992, Updated 10 December 1993.* [Miami]: National Hurricane Center, 1993. 38 pp.

Redland Conservancy/1000 Friends of Florida. *After Andrew: Conservation Opportunities and Challenges in South Dade—An Environmental Summit. Conference Proceedings.* Princeton, Fla.: Redland Conservancy, 1994–96.

Region VI Interagency Hazard Mitigation Team. *Hazard Mitigation Report: In Response to the August 26, 1992 Disaster Declaration, State of Louisiana, FEMA-956-DR-LA,* Washington D.C.: [Federal Emergency Management Agency?]. 26 pp.

Riad, Jasmin. "Relocation, Housing Conditions, and Psychological Distress Following Hurricane Andrew." Master's thesis, Georgia State University, 1994. 64 leaves.

Rice, Michael Dean. "Woody Debris Decomposition in the Atchafalaya River Basin of South Louisiana Following Hurricane Andrew." Master's thesis, Auburn University, 1997. 96 leaves.

Risi, John Andrew. "Event Sedimentations from Hurricane Andrew along the Southwest Florida Coast." Ph.D. diss., University of Miami, 1998. 199 pp.

Robert R. Rosen Associates. *Hurricane Andrew Damage, South Dade Plaza, Homestead, Fla.: Structural Engineering Inspection Report.* Conshohocken, Pa.: Robert R. Rosen Associates, 1993.

Rodriguez, Mario S. "The Role of Optimism and Coping in Immune and Neuroendocrine Responses and Physical Health in the Aftermath of Hurricane Andrew." Ph.D. diss., University of Miami, 1995. 226 leaves.

Rosenstiel School of Marine and Atmospheric Science. *Research on the Environmental Consequences and Recovery Processes from Hurricane Andrew.* Miami: Rosenstiel School of Marine and Atmospheric Science, University of Miami, 1993. 17 pp.

Ross, Jimmy D. *The Role of the U.S. Army Materiel Command, Logistics Support Group in the Hurricane Andrew Relief Operations.* [Adelphi, Md.?]: U.S. Army Materiel Command, 1995.

Royal Bahamas Defense Force. *Defender: The Royal Bahamas Defence Force Magazine.* Nassau: Royal Bahamas Defense Force, 1993. 92 pp.

Rupp, William Thomas. "Toward a Process Model of Corporate Social Performance in Response to Natural Disasters: An Analysis of Corporate America's Response to Hurricane Andrew." Ph.D. diss., University of Georgia, 1994. 336 leaves.

Salyer, Michael R. "Assessment of Hurricane Andrew Damage to White-Tailed Deer Habitat in Forested Wetlands in Louisiana." Master's thesis, Louisiana State University, 1995. 58 pp.

Schumacher, Lois M. "An Exploration in Juvenile Post-Traumatic Stress Disorder as a Consequence of a Natural Disaster: A Preliminary Study." Ph.D. diss., Union Institute, 1996. 104 pp.

[Scottish Association of Geography Teachers]. *Earth Forces.* N.p.: [Scottish Association of Geography Teachers], 1994. 1 pack.

Shelby, Janine S. "Crisis Intervention with Children Following Hurricane Andrew: A Comparison of Two Treatment Approaches." Ph.D. diss., University of Miami, 1994. 128 leaves.

Sherrow, Victoria. *Hurricane Andrew: Nature's Rage*. Springfield, N.J.: Enslow, 1998. 48 pp.

Smart, A. C. *Military Support to Domestic Disaster Relief: Doctrine for Operating in the Wake of the Enemy?* Fort Leavenworth, Kansas: School of Advanced Military Studies, U.S. Army Command and General Staff College, 1993. 64 pp.

Smith, F. G. Walton. *Anatomy of a Hurricane: An Inside Look at the Planet's Powerhouse*. New York: Nature America / International Oceanographic Foundation, 1992. [5 pp.]

Society of Civil Engineers. *Hurricanes of 1992, "Andrew and Iniki One Year Later": Proceedings of a Symposium, December 1–3, 1993*. Miami: Society of Civil Engineers, 1993.

South Florida History Magazine: Special Hurricane Issue. 1992. 31 pp.

Steffen, Patrick R. "Anger and Health in Context: The Impact of a Traumatic Natural Disaster on the Relationship between Anger and Health." Master's thesis, University of Miami, 1996. 115 leaves.

———. "Optimism and Psychological and Physiological Well-Being Following a Natural Disaster." Ph.D. diss., University of Miami, 1998. 122 pp.

Stuetzle, Rick E. "Substance Use in the Aftermath of Hurricane Andrew." Master's thesis, University of Miami, 1996. 119 leaves.

Tait, Lawrence S., comp. *Lessons of Hurricane Andrew: Excerpts from the 15th Annual National Hurricane Conference*. Washington, D.C.: Federal Emergency Management Agency, 1993. 92 pp.

Torres, Angela Robin. "Effects of Hurricane Andrew on Cavity-Nesting Birds in the Lower Atchafalaya River Basin." Master's thesis, University of Southwestern Louisiana, 1995. 98 leaves.

U.S. Army Corps of Engineers. *Headquarters USACE After Action Report for Hurricane Andrew and Iniki*. [Washington, D.C.]: U.S. Army Corps of Engineers, 1993.

———. Jacksonville District, Central and Southern Florida Project, Dade County, Florida. *Plans for Hurricane Andrew Rehabilitation of Levee 31 E System*. Jacksonville: Corps of Engineers, 1992. 31 leaves.

———. Jacksonville District. *Hurricane Andrew, After Action Report*. Jacksonville: Corps of Engineers, 1993. 432 pp.

U.S. Department of Commerce. National Oceanic and Atmospheric Administration. *NOAA in the News, Weekly Clippings from Newspapers and Magazines across the Country: Local and National Articles about Hurricane Andrew and the Performance of NOAA's National Weather Service*. Washington D.C.: U.S. Department of Commerce, 1992.

———. National Oceanic and Atmospheric Administration. *North American Climate Advisory Update 92/2: Tropical Summary Growing Season Conditions, Drought Impact Outlook*. Washington, D.C.: U.S. Dept of Commerce, 1992. 23 pp.

———. National Oceanic and Atmospheric Administration. National Weather Ser-

vice. *Hurricane Andrew: South Florida and Louisiana: August 23–26, 1992.* Silver
Spring, Md.: National Weather Service, 1993. 1 vol.

———. National Oceanic and Atmospheric Administration. Ocean Products Center.
Surface and Near-Surface Marine Observations during Hurricane Andrew. Washington, D.C.: U.S. Department of Commerce, 1993. 37 pp.

U.S. Department of Energy. *When Disaster Strikes, the Sun Can Still Shine Through.*
[Washington, D.C.]: U.S. Department of Energy, 1994. 1 folded sheet.

U.S. Department of Housing and Urban Development. *"Hurricane Andrew: One Year
Later": Status Report on Federal Assistance.* Washington, D.C.: U.S. Department of
Housing and Urban Development, 1993. 23 pp.

———. *Hurricane Andrew's Effect on Manufactured Housing in Florida and Louisiana.*
[Washington, D.C.]: U.S. Department of Housing and Urban Development,
1992. 24 pp.

———. Office of Policy Development and Research. *Assessment of Damage to Single-
Family Homes Caused by Hurricanes Andrew and Iniki.* Washington, D.C.: U.S.
Department of Housing and Urban Development, 1993. 112 pp.

U.S. Department of the Interior. National Park Service. *Effects of Hurricane Andrew on
Natural and Archeological Resources: Big Cypress National Preserve, Biscayne National Park, and Everglades National Park.* Denver: U.S. Department of the Interior,
1996. 150 pp.

U.S. House Committee on Banking, Finance, and Urban Affairs. Subcommittee on
Consumer Credit and Insurance. *The Availability of Insurance in Areas at Risk of
Natural Disasters: Field Hearing before the Subcommittee on Consumer Credit and
Insurance.* Washington, D.C.: GPO, 1994. 327 pp.

U.S. House Committee on Veterans' Affairs. Subcommittee on Housing and Memorial Affairs. *Hurricane Andrew—VA Housing and Homelessness, Homestead, Florida: Field Hearing Before the Subcommittee on Housing and Memorial Affairs.* Washington, D.C.: GPO, 1993. 113 pp.

U.S. Nuclear Regulatory Commission. *Effect of Hurricane Andrew on the Turkey Point
Nuclear Generating Station from August 20–30, 1992.* Washington D.C.: U.S.
Nuclear Regulatory Commission, 1993.

———. Office of the Secretary. *Amendment to Memorandum of Understanding
(MOU) Between the Federal Emergency Agency (FEMA) and the Nuclear Regulatory
Commission (NRC) Based on Lessons Learned from Hurricane Andrew.* Washington,
D.C.: U.S. Nuclear Regulatory Commission, 1993. 14 pp.

U.S. President. *Requests for Supplemental Appropriations, Communication from the
President of the United States Transmitting Requests for Fiscal Year 1993 Emergency
Appropriations Language for the Departments of Housing and Urban Development
and the Interior to Provide Housing Assistance in Florida, Louisiana, Hawaii, and
Guam to Victims of Hurricanes Andrew and Iniki and Typhoon Omar, and Support to
Louisiana in Studying and Repairing Ecological Damage Caused by Hurricane Andrew, Pursuant to Public Law 102–368, Chapter 10 (106 Stat. 1158).* Washington:
GPO, 1993. 6 pp.

U.S. Senate Committee on Environment and Public Works. Subcommittee on Toxic Substances, Research, and Development. *Lessons Learned from Hurricane Andrew: Hearing before the Subcommittee on Environment and Research, and Development.* Washington, D.C.: GPO, 1993. 1337 pp.

U.S. Veterans Health Administration. Emergency Medical Preparedness Office. *Hurricane Andrew After-Action Report.* Washington, D.C.: GPO, 1993. 100 pp.

Villanueva, Maria L., and Donald W. Pybas, eds. *Recommendations for Hurricane Preparations and Responses for Boating Communities and Industries.* Gainesville: Florida Sea Grant College Program, University of Florida, 1994. 70 pp.

Vincent, Nicole Renee. "Children's Responses to Natural Disasters: Role of Academic Achievement." Master's thesis, University of Miami, 1995. 84 leaves.

———. "Children's Reactions to Hurricane Andrew: A Forty-Four Month Follow-Up Study (Natural Disasters, Posttraumatic Stress Disorder, Trauma)." Ph.D. diss., University of Miami, 1997. 130 pp.

Vogel, Richard Michael. "Regional Growth, Structural Change, and Natural Disaster (Hurricane Florida)." Ph.D. diss., Florida International University, 1996. 279 pp.

Wagner, Stacy Ellen. "The Relationship of Optimism and Self-Efficacy to the Psychological, Physiological, and Health Status of HIV+ Gay Men in the Face of a Natural Disaster and Two Years Later." Master's thesis, University of Miami, 1996. 222 leaves.

Wang, Hsiang. *Andrew Versus Hugo: Damages to Residential Communities.* Gainesville: Coastal and Oceanographic Engineering Department, University of Florida, 1993. 62 pp.

Wassertein, Shari Beth. "The Relationships between Marital Discord, Peer Support, Hurricane Severity, and Children's Behavior." Master's thesis, University of Miami, 1993. 64 leaves.

Winter, Nancy Lesson. "Managing a Mega-Disaster: GIS Applications, Decision-Making, and Spatial Data Flow Between Local, State, and Federal Levels in Hurricane Andrew Disaster Management." Ph.D. diss., Clark University, 1997. 310 pp.

Wynings, Christian Gierlotka. "The Role of Social Support, Financial Resources, and Living Situation in the Initial Impact of, and Recovery from, Hurricane Andrew." Master's thesis, University of Miami, 1994. 188 leaves.

———. "The Interaction of Depression, Anxiety, and Social Support in Predicting Long-Term Distress in Victims of Hurricane Andrew." Ph.D. diss., University of Miami, 1997. 225 pp.

Ying, Jun. "Development and Verification of Computer Simulation Models for Evaluation of Siting Strategies and Evacuation Procedures for Mobile Drilling Units in Hurricanes (Gulf of Mexico)." Ph.D. diss., University of California, Berkeley, 1996. 223 pp.

Zollo, Ronald F. *Hurricane Andrew: August 24, 1992—Structural Performance of Buildings in Dade County, Florida.* Coral Gables: University of Miami, 1993. 69 pp.

Audiovisual Materials

A Consumers' Guide to Homeowners' Insurance. [Tallahassee]: Florida Department of Insurance, 1994. Videocassette (12 min.): col., 1/2 in.

The Aftermath of Hurricane Andrew. Silver Spring, Md.: ADRA International, 1992. Videocassette: col., 1/2 in.

Andrew. [Miami]: WSVN-TV, 1992. Videocassette (105 min.): sd. col., 1/2 in.

Back from Disaster. Jacksonville: Blue Cross/Blue Shield of Florida, 1993. Videocassette: col., 1/2 in.

Emergency Planning: The Big Picture for Water Utilities. Denver: American Water Works Association, 1995. Videocassette (28 min.): col., 1/2 in.

Exploring Storm Surge. Tampa: U.S. Geological Survey, 1995. Videocassette (14 min.): 1/2 in.

Eye of the Storm. Tampa: WTVT, 1993. Videocassette (ca. 40 min.): col., 1/2 in.

First Report, Hurricane Andrew; Chemical Plant Fire, Odessa, TX; Multiple Shooting, North Dade County, FL; 2d Alarm: Part I, Underwater Rescue Training; Los Angeles Riots Update. St. Louis: American Heat Video Productions, 1992. Videocassette (51 min.): col., 1/2 in.

Fly Over of Debris Sites Showing Their Present Status. Jacksonville: The District, 1993. Videocassette (53 min.): col., 1/2 in.

Great Weather Catastrophes. Atlanta: Weather Channel, 1993 and 1994. Videocassette (40 min.): col., with black-and-white sequences, 1/2 in.; guide.

Hurricane! Cineworks, in association with WGBH Boston and BBC TV, for NOVA. Princeton, N.J.: Films for the Humanities, 1993. Videocassette (58 min.): 1/2 in.

Hurricane! An Event-Based Science Module. Meteorology Module. Menlo Park, Calif.: Innovative Learning Publications, Addison-Wesley, 1995. Videocassette (15 min.): col., 1/2 in.

Hurricane Andrew. Miami: Richard Horodner, 1992. Videocassette (54 min.): col., 1/2 in.

Hurricane Andrew: A Slide Presentation with Commentary. Capitol Heights, Md.: National Audiovisual Center, 1993. 111 slides.

Hurricane Andrew, August 1992: Satellite and Radar Sequences. Madison: University of Wisconsin, 1992. Videocassette (12 min.): col., 1/2 in.

Hurricane Andrew COE Recovery Orientation Reminders. Jacksonville: The District, 1992. Videocassette (12 min.): col., 1/2 in.

Hurricane Andrew Disaster Recovery. South Florida Chapter of the EDPAA, Florida Atlantic University, and Eta Tau chapter of Beta Alpha Psi. Boca Raton: Florida Atlantic University, 1994. Videocassette (59 min.).

Hurricane Andrew Hits Monkey Jungle. Miami: Monkey Jungle, 1992. Videocassette (13 min.): col., 1/2 in.

Hurricane Andrew Live on Video. Miami: Richard Horodner, 1992. Videocassette (54 min.): col., 1/2 in.

Hurricane Andrew Recovery "Toward the Light." Jacksonville: The District, 1993. Videocassette (19 min.): col., 1/2 in.

Hurricane Andrew's Swath. Oak Forest, Ill.: MPI Home Video, 1992. Videocassette (23 min.): col., 1/2 in.

Hurricane Force: A Coastal Perspective. Department of the Interior, U.S. Geological Survey, 1994. Videorecording (29 min.): col., 1/2 in.

Hurricanes: Natural Born Killers. [New York]: History Channel, 1996. Videocassette (47 min.): col., 1/2 in.

Indiana Guardsman Video Magazine. N.p.: n.p., 1992. Videocassette: col., 1/2 in.

Jack Hanna's Animal Adventures: Wake-Up Call. Glastonbury, Conn.: VideoTours, 1994. Videocassette (VHS, 20 min.): sd. (stereo), col., 1/2 in.

Lessons Learned from Hurricane Andrew. Parts 1 and 2. Miami: Florida International University, 1993. 2 videocassettes (28 min. ea.): col., 1/2 in.

Lessons Learned from Hurricane Andrew: A Conference Sponsored by Florida International University. 1993. Miami: Florida International University. 29 videocassettes (50–90 min. ea.): col., 1/2 in.

Like a Mighty Wind. Wescosville, Pa.: ELCA Inter-Lutheran Disaster Response, 1992. Videocassette (13 min.): col., 1/2 in.

Love Is What We've Got; Con Amor. N.p.: Marsal Enterprises, 1992. Sound cassette: analog.

Monsters of the Deep. [Oak Park, Ill.]: MPI Home Video, 1996. Videocassette (ca. 57 min.): col., with black-and-white sequences, 1/2 in.

Nature's Fury. Culver City, Calif.: Columbia Tristar Home Video, 1996. Videocassette (60 min.): col., with black-and-white sequences, 1/2 in.

Norcross, Brian. *Hurricane Andrew as It Happened.* [Miami]: WTVJ, 1992. Videocassette.

Out of Andrew's Shadow. Juno Beach, Fla.: FPL Corporate Communications, 1992. Videocassette (36 min.): col., 1/2 in.

Surviving the Hurricane. Miami: WPBT Productions, 1993. Videocassette (58 min.): col., 1/2 in.

Tracking the Storm. Miami: WTVJ, 1992. Videocassette (15 min.): col., 1/2 in.

U.S. Army JTF Andrew Overview. [Ft. Bragg, S.C.]: 22nd Mobile Public Affairs Detachment, 1993. Videocassette (5 min.): col., 1/2 in.

Viewing Geography, a CNN Global Perspective. N.p.: Turner Multimedia, Cable News Network, 1992. Videocassette (45 min.): col., 1/2 in.; with teachers' guide and 6 blackline masters.

Wessells, Steve. *Hurricane Force: A Coastal Perspective.* N.p.: U.S. Department of the Interior, U.S. Geological Survey, 1994. Videorecording.

The Wind of Change. Stamford, Conn.: Carvill America, 1994. Videocassette (55 min.): col., 1/2 in.; with pamphlet.

Windows on Science. Update, vol. 3. Warren, N.J.: The Corporation, 1994. Videodisc: col., 8 in.; with 6 update guides.

The Year the Sky Fell. Atlanta: BVE Products/Weather Channel, 1994. Videocassette (38 min.): col., 1/2 in.

Maps

Coast Watch [Hurricane Andrew and Hurricane Iniki]. Coastal Ocean Program. Rockville, Md.: U.S. Department of Commerce, National Oceanic and Atmospheric Administration, 1992. 8 maps.

Damage Map of Hurricane Andrew. Miami: U.S. Department of Commerce, National Oceanic and Atmospheric Administration, Atlantic Oceanographic and Meteorological Laboratories, 1992. 2 maps.

Damage Map of Hurricane Andrew on August 24, 1992. Chicago: University of Chicago, 1992. 5 maps.

Damage Zones, Hurricane Andrew, August 24, 1992. South Dade County, Fla.: N.p., 1992. 1 map.

Distribution Centers, Hurricane Andrew, August 24, 1992. South Dade County, Fla.: N.p., 1992. 1 map.

Dymon, Ute J. *Map Use During and After Hurricane Andrew.* Boulder: National Hazards Research and Applications Center, University of Colorado, 1993. 10pp.

Hurricane Andrew, NWS Miami Radar, 24 August 1992, 08:36 UTC, 04:35 EDT. Miami: U.S. Department of Commerce, National Oceanic and Atmospheric Administration, Hurricane Research Division, 1992. 1 map.

Hurricane Andrew, 24 August 1992, 5 am edt, 145 mph. Miami: U.S. Dept of Commerce, National Oceanic and Atmospheric Administration, National Hurricane Center, 1992. 3 maps.

Hurricane Debris Curbside Collection. Metropolitan Dade County. Miami: Department of Solid Waste Management, 1992. 1 map.

Red Cross Housing Damage Assessment Associated with Hurricane Andrew. Southern Dade County, Fla. [Miami?]: N.p., 1992. 1 map.

Storm Surge Associated with Hurricane Andrew, August 24, 1992. N.p.: N.p., 1992. 1 map.

Index

Military (Army, Marines), 62–64, 72, 86, 132–33
Miller Drive (Southwest 56th Street), 62
Modernage, 114
Mold and mildew after Andrew, 109–10
Monkey Jungle, 110
Monroe County, Fla., 62
Mooney, James, 4–5, 97, 104
Moore Haven, Fla., 2
Moose, Lawrence, 5–6, 15, 24, 42–43, 68–69, 104
Moss, Amy, 72

Naranja, 38
National Emergency Medical Team, 59, 60
National Guard, 46, 53, 56–57, 58–61, 63–64, 72, 120
National Hurricane Center (Miami), xiii–xiv, 2, 13, 14
Nine-one-one, 26
Nirscel, Roy, 78
Norcross, Bryan, 5, 11, 14, 18–19, 29–31, 32, 123
North Kendall Drive (Southwest 88th Street), 43, 46, 56, 87, 88, 122
Nova Southern, 114–15
Nursery and foliage plant industry, 107–8

Oldiges, Mary, 138
152nd Street, 39, 98
196th Street, 98
Opa Locka Airport, 61–62
Overtown, Fla., 92

Palmer-Trinity School, 61
Palmetto Expressway, 46, 86
Palmetto General Hospital, 64
Parker, Ginger, 114
Parrot Jungle, 10, 110
Peaches Record Store, 53, 62
Pembroke Pines Hospital, 102
Perdue Medical Center, 12
Perez, Pablo E., 107–8
Pernick, Vida, 3, 123–24, 125
Perrine, Fla., 31, 38, 56, 67
Pest control after Andrew, 108–9
Piet, Dan, 38

Pivnik, Sheldon, 86
Plantation, Fla., 88
Police, and Hurricane Andrew: help from South Carolina officers after, 52; looting after, 56, 57; preparations for, 23; relief/rescue operations after, 52–55; traditional role of, redefined after, 54
Politics and politicians, xi, 52, 58, 61–62, 65, 89–90
Ponton, Ronald V., 7, 67, 68, 91
Porobic, Nora, 121–22
Pregnant women, 11–12
Price gouging, xi, 84–86
Promenade Plaza, 56
Puller, Mike, 9, 37

Quintairos, Cristina, 25

Real estate, after Andrew, 123–26
Red Cross, American (national), 42, 52, 68, 88
Red Cross, Greater Miami Chapter, 5–6, 15, 24, 42, 68–69, 104
Redlands, Fla., 93
Redondo Elementary School, 133–34
Reece, Greg, 84–85
Reece, Michael, 84–85
Rhodes, 114
Richardson, Master Sgt. Lester, 63
Richmond Heights, Fla., 44, 47, 68, 132
"Roofers from hell," xi, 118–21
Ros-Lehtinen, Congresswoman Ileana, 62
Rumors, 86

Saga Bay, Fla., 126
Sailboat Bay (Coconut Grove), 32
Salvation Army, 70
Santelices, Armando, 64
Sardinas, Tony, 70
Schorle, Suzanne, 94, 125, 138–39
Schulz, Peter, 36
Scott, LaWanda, 97, 139
Seavers, Scott, 30
Shaffer, Laurie, 128
Shaffer, Paul, 8, 10–11, 48–50, 127–28
Shaw, John, 133
Sheets, Bob, 2

Eugene F. Provenzo, Jr., has been since 1976 a professor in the School of Education at the University of Miami. The author of a wide range of books on educational and social issues, his work has been reviewed in the *New York Times*, *The Guardian*, *Mother Jones*, the *Wall Street Journal*, and the *London Economist*. His book *Farm Security Administration Photographs of Florida* (University Press of Florida, 1993), coauthored with Michael Carlebach, was selected by the American Association for State and Local History as an outstanding book in the field of state and local history.

Asterie Baker Provenzo has pursued graduate work in architectural history at the University of Miami. She is a widely published author and curriculum developer.

Books of Related Interest Available from University Press of Florida

Florida Hurricanes and Tropical Storms, 1871–2001, Expanded Edition,
   by John M. Williams and Iver W. Duedall
Florida Weather, by Morton D. Winsberg
Atlas of Florida, edited by Edward A. Fernald and Elizabeth Purdum
Castles in the Sand: The Life and Times of Carl Graham Fisher, by
   Mark S. Foster
Miami, U.S.A.: Expanded Edition, by Helen Muir
Florida: A Short History, by Michael Gannon